the lotus effect

shedding suffering
and rediscovering
your essential self

PAVEL G. SOMOV, PH.D.

New Harbinger Publications, Inc.

Publisher's Note

This publication is designed to provide accurate and authoritative information in regard to the subject matter covered. It is sold with the understanding that the publisher is not engaged in rendering psychological, financial, legal, or other professional services. If expert assistance or counseling is needed, the services of a competent professional should be sought.

Distributed in Canada by Raincoast Books

Copyright © 2010 by Pavel G. Somov
New Harbinger Publications, Inc.
5674 Shattuck Avenue
Oakland, CA 94609
www.newharbinger.com

Acquired by Melissa Kirk; Cover design by Amy Shoup; Edited by Carole Honeychurch

Library of Congress Cataloging-in-Publication Data

Somov, Pavel G.
   The Lotus effect : shedding suffering and rediscovering your essential self / Pavel G. Somov.
      p. cm.
   Includes bibliographical references.
   ISBN 978-1-57224-919-6 (print) -- ISBN 978-1-57224-920-2 (pdf) 1. Suffering. 2. Suffering--Religious aspects--Buddhism. 3.   Worry--Religious aspects--Buddhism. 4. Self-perception. I. Title.
   BF789.S8S66 2010
   294.3'4442--dc22
                                   2010028046

17 16 15

10 9 8 7 6 5 4 3

To Thich Quang Duc*, who knew what he was and what he wasn't even while on fire.

* Thich Quang Duc, a sixty-six-year-old Buddhist monk, immolated himself on June 11, 1963, in protest of the persecution of Buddhists in South Vietnam. "As he burned, he never moved a muscle, never uttered a sound, his outward composure in sharp contrast to the wailing people around him" (Halberstam, 211).

contents

PART 3

Re-Identify with What You Are

PART 4

Perennial Growth

lotus identity

CHAPTER 1

the lotus effect

*Do not go to the garden of flowers! O friend! Go not there.
In your body is the garden of flowers. Take your seat on the
thousand petals of the lotus, and there gaze on the infinite
beauty.*

Kabir

*I love the lotus because, while growing from the mud, it is
unstained.*

Zhou Dunvi

What is identity, and what is difference?

Chandrakirti

In the spring of 1951, horticulturist Dr. George Harding of the
National Capital Parks was astonished to see that two lotus plants
had sprouted in his Washington, DC, greenhouse (Time Magazine
1951). He knew very well how the lotus seeds had gotten there; what
was so surprising to Dr. Harding was that these seeds had actually

germinated. After all, the seeds, which had been picked out of the sediment of an ancient lake in northeastern China, were claimed to be 50,000 years old (Shen-Miller et al. 2002; Time Magazine 1951).

That claim was a bit exaggerated; still, these particular seeds had lain dormant for an incredibly long time before proving they remained viable. Indeed, they won the seed longevity record: other seeds from the same batch, collected in the 1920s by a Japanese botanist named Ichiro Ohga, were revealed by carbon dating to be about a whopping 1,300 years old (Shen-Miller et al. 2002). That meant that each of the lotus seeds that had just come to life in 1951 was a "relic of one of the early crops of lotus cultivated by Buddhists" after the introduction of Buddhism to the region—Pulantien, Liaoning province—where they were found (Shen-Miller et al. 1995, 1367).

Had we been standing next to Dr. Harding when he witnessed those lotuses bloom, marveling at the showy, dish-like leaves and the beautiful pink of the lotus corolla rising gracefully above the surface of the water, we might have thought: "how is it possible for a living thing to remain itself, unaffected amidst the mud of its circumstance, for such a long, long time?" It is exactly this question of identity that preoccupied Chandrakirti, the seventh-century Buddhist thinker who happened to die around the very time Dr. Harding's lotus seeds were produced. Indeed, what *is* identity? What is essence? What is purity? What is self? Or are these questions just different ways of looking at the same issue? Perhaps, but let's not get ahead of ourselves.

In the 1970s German botanist Wilhelm Barthlott studied *Nelumbo nucifera* (the Sacred Lotus) through a scanning electron microscope (Barthlott and Neinhuis 1997). The reason for his interest had to do with an amazing property of the lotus leaves: they are self-cleaning! Indeed, the lotus leaves are extremely water repellent (*superhydrophobic*, in technical parlance). Water droplets roll right off the leaves, washing away any dirt particles. As a result, the lotus, an aquatic flower that starts out at the muddy bottom, manages to rise to the water's surface unstained and free of the muck of its humble origins.

the lotus: metaphor for personal integrity

The sacred lotus offers an inspiring rags-to-riches, slime-to-sunshine metaphor of growth and enlightenment. We might consider the lotus to be the ultimate Cinderella story: it cleans all day and never gets dirty. The self-cleaning lotus exemplifies an empowering narrative of integrity. It manages to remain *itself*, pure and unaffected, and to grow to its fullest amidst the impurity of its circumstance. Unsurprisingly, the lotus flower (*padma* in Sanskrit) has a position of great cultural and spiritual significance in Asia. In Buddhism, the lotus represents purification and disentanglement from the trappings of conditioned existence (*samsara*), liberation from suffering, and the achievement of enlightenment. The cross-legged "lotus pose" (*padm'asana*) in yoga is a universally recognizable symbol of wisdom and serenity. As a visual symbol, the lotus flower is inescapable: it is a core element of Asian iconography. As a sound, the lotus invocation is forever resonated in the *om mani padma hum* mantra ("jewel in the lotus").

As intriguing as this scientific and cultural lotus trivia might be, this book, of course, isn't about the bio-mimetic (nature-mimicking) nano-technological applications of the lotus effect; nor is this book about sitting in the lotus asana. This book is about a psychological kind of lotus effect; namely, about surviving the informational muck that constantly bogs us down.

Case in point: you wake up feeling good. You step up on the bathroom scale and see a number that you don't like. Suddenly, your mood goes down the drain. What happened? Technically, nothing happened: you—in your essence—are still exactly the same as you were before you weighed yourself. The only difference is that now you have a toxic piece of information on your mind: a number. A moment ago you were feeling fine, but now this informational tidbit is eating at you.

As banal as this case of informational poisoning is, it shows the potent toxicity of information. This basic scenario is the story of

5

many lives. Whether you gain a pound, lose your car keys, fail a test, pass gas in public, have a bad hair day, or get a good administrative lashing, your brain continuously translates life into information, and this information transforms how you feel about your essence. Information disrupts our hard-won calmness with the ease of a stone skipping across a sleepy pond. The number on your bathroom scale is just a tiny pebble, but look at the (emotional) waves it makes! The goal of this book is to help you thicken your psychological skin and teach you how to shed the informational dirt, lotus-like. I'm not talking about ignoring information—that wouldn't be helpful. What I'd like to explore with you is the very real possibility of healing from the toxic information that wounds our sense of self. This book is about surviving this stream of information, about not getting drowned in it. Our goal will be to remain in our essence, unaffected, unstained, and free, cultivating a lotus-like capacity for self-cleaning from the informational residue that stands in the way of our growth and well-being. In sum, this book is about cultivating *the lotus effect*—the skill of informational detoxification—and about rediscovering the lotus of your essential self.

Informational Traces

Remember Ichiro Ohga, the Japanese botanist whose lotus seeds Dr. Harding sprouted in his greenhouse? Well, there's a relevant backstory to this. The seeds might have been actually collected by someone else. In the 1920s the Japanese occupied northeastern China, and Ohga employed the assistance of a local Chinese farmer named Liu (Shen-Miller et al. 2002). Liu was responsible for the fieldwork and collected most of the lotus seeds. My guess is that Liu didn't mind this botanical treasure hunt at all. Chances are it was a good, well-paying gig and an intriguing opportunity to catch a glimpse of the historical dimension of his ancestral village of Liujia Zhuang. Later, however, when the Chinese authorities learned that Liu had collaborated with a Japanese official, he was executed. A one-time profitable affiliation suddenly became a fatal liability.

That's the way it goes. Affiliations, attachments, and identifications leave an informational trace, both inside and outside of us. And information—to the extent to which it misrepresents, mischaracterizes, and misidentifies us—is dirt. Working with Dr. Ohga did not make Liu into a Japanese collaborator. This work was simply the action of finding lotus seeds—an action Liu performed, not something he *was*. He was not his actions.

Apparently, this was too subtle a distinction for his accusers, and the information about Liu's actions fatally defined his essence. This is an all-too-common phenomenon: information about a given life becomes more important than the life itself. This book is a call to change this ingrained and toxic habit of confusing information about ourselves with the essence of who we are. So, before we move on, let us remember Liu and the countless others for their essence and not for the information that buried them. Let us recognize that a lotus seed isn't the dirt in which it's buried.

A Walk Down the Garden Path

Before you roll up your sleeves and begin cultivating your lotus identity, let me offer you a brief overview of this growth endeavor of ours. First, in chapter 2, we'll sow a handful of lotus seeds. After all, a harvest of self begins with seeds of self-reflection. We'll also prep and prime, cultivate and aerate the soil of your consciousness with the discussion of what I call "identity detox." Then, in chapter 3, we'll get down and dirty by beginning to weed out what we are not from the lotus of what we are (via a process of "dis-identification"). In chapter 4 we'll take steps to protect your budding lotus identity from the scorching sun of nihilism. Then, in chapter 5 we'll further cultivate the lotus of your essential self with the help of "re-identification" exercises. Chapter 6 brings us to the ways in which your lotus self may join the all-pervading blossom of global consciousness. While the first three parts of this book (chapters 2 through 5) are self-help psychology, chapter 6 will help you explore an ancient existential self-view with deep spiritual and philosophical roots. In chapter 7, we'll finish by taking a tour of the identity-detox emergency room that you might visit in the future should you lose sight of your essential self.

CHAPTER 2

identity detox

Life begins by emptying oneself.

Ilchi Lee

The perfect person employs mind as a mirror. It grasps nothing; it refuses nothing; it receives, but does not keep.

Zhuangzi

The goal of this book is to help you shift from ego identity to lotus identity. I define *ego* as an informational snapshot of ourselves that we have internalized from our interactions with the environment. As such, ego is a false self. In its dependence on the external, in its attachment to reflection, in its grasping for validation, in its clinging to approval, ego identity gathers a lot of informational dirt. Lotus identity is different: it is self-referencing and, thus, self-cleaning. Like a lotus leaf or the impenetrable, reflective surface of a mirror, lotus identity repels toxic information and remains unsullied and pristine. But to claim and retain your lotus identity, you will need to shed the effluvia of the ego. This process is what I call *identity detox*.

Identity detox is a process of peeling away your false self, one layer of false identity at a time. While leaving your ego identity behind may sometimes feel like a loss, it's anything but. Each and every time you strip away another layer of false identity, you reveal, bit by bit, your true self. As each level of informational artifice falls away, you gain a degree of freedom. As such, identity detox is a process of liberating you from the information that stands in the way of your growth.

plant a lotus seed: draw a boundary

Grab a sheet of paper and a pencil. (A pen won't do—you'll understand why later). Now draw a large circle. Label the inside of the circle as "I" or "Me." Label the area outside the circle as "Not-I" or "Not-Me." The line of the circle is the boundary of your self.

Look around you. Look inside you. Think about your life. Ponder what constitutes your sense of self. Ask yourself: what makes me me? How do I know myself from my environment? What am I?

Inside the circle, write down whatever you feel is *inalienable* to your essence. Define your self. As you go through this process, keep asking yourself if any given aspect of your self is actually essential. Rule of thumb: if you can live without it, it's not you. Leave what you are not outside. Document this itemized self-description by making notes inside the circle. When you have finalized your definition of self, begin to symbolically reinforce the boundary between *you* and *not-you* by tracing the circle line over and over until the pencil tears all the way through the paper, until you effectively separate what you think you are from what you are not. Note that your take on this exercise is likely to change as you read on. So, hold on to this piece of paper as a reference point.

identity theft and identity giveaway

Identity theft is when someone identifies themselves as you and steals your resources. *Identity giveaway* is when you identify as someone else and surrender your sense of individuality and uniqueness. All identification with the external is a giveaway of your essence.

The word "identity" comes from the Latin word *idem,* which means "same." Identity is built through identification with the external, with what you are not. We determine our identities by comparing ourselves to "not-ourselves" and thereby try to determine who we are. We tend to think along the lines of "I am like this or that" or "I am like so-and-so or such-and-such." Therein lies the problem.

You aren't like anything or anybody else, even if you are similar. Similarity isn't sameness. No one is the same as you. Number 1.0000001 is very, very close to 1, but it still isn't a true 1. Only 1 is 1. And only you are you. There is no one like you. You are not an almost-you, or a kinda-you, or a sorta-you. You are one of a kind, fully and *uniquely* you! When we identify (equate) ourselves with the external, with what is not us, we ignore the very uniqueness that makes us different. Recognize that uniqueness is beyond comparison. Recognize that you are beyond comparison. Recognize that as long as you define what you are by what you are not, you are exchanging your uniqueness and oneness for similarity. And, in so doing, you are giving away your identity and losing sight of your essential, unique self. Identification with the external is an identity giveaway. Identity giveaway, just like identity theft, is a loss of self.

Identification Is an Information-Attachment Problem

So, why is it that we give away our essence, exchanging the original for a copy? The answer is complex, nuanced, and case-specific, but here's a bird's-eye view of the problem. You see, the brain translates life into information. Some of the information that we receive has nothing to do with us. We either ignore it or file it away for future use. But some of the information feels personally relevant. So, we examine it and hoard what's useful. The information that we keep becomes our ego, our self-concept.

Over time, we get used to this information about us and begin to identify with it. For example, you get a few As in a graduate-level math class, and you feel tempted to conclude: "I am a math whiz." Or, let's say that you grow up in a coal-mining town, identifying with its ethos of honesty and hard work, and then run for a political office as "a son of a coal miner" with a promise of what-you-see-is-what-you-get transparence. One way or another, we all wrap ourselves in our informational and autobiographical résumés until they cake on like a second skin. But life, nevertheless, continues. Things change. And new informational input eventually challenges our self-concept. You finally get a B on a math test and your self-coronated math-whiz title suddenly needs a revision; or a sensation-hungry tabloid finally data-mines something shady on the goody-two-shoes, what-you-see-is-what-you-get son of a coal miner, and another political ascent nose-dives. One way or another we all lose our informational halo.

Our usual way of dealing with information we don't like is to ignore it, to question its validity, to question the validity of its source, or to counter it with other information. We get pretty stressed out trying to protect the old information about who and what we are. We go to bat protecting our image, our reputation, our self-view, our ego, while all along forgetting that what we're protecting is just information. We lose sight of a rather basic fact that we, ourselves, are not the information that we are protecting.

This book isn't about disregarding or dismissing negative information. Chances are you already have these information-filtering self-defense skills. We are going to take an entirely different path, the path of dis-identifying from information altogether. What you have here is an opportunity to draw a boundary between *you* and *the informa-tion about you*. Once you latch on to a certain set of ideas about who and what you are, you end up identifying with this informa-tion. And as this information becomes your identity, you lose sight of your essential self. Identity detox isn't the dry-cleaning of identity. It's not a reputation mop-up. It's not a do-it-yourself image-management project or a self-esteem tune-up. Identity detox is a process of liberat-ing you (your essential self) from the information about you (from your informational ego).

the ego-self: identification, information, impermanence

Ego is not an anatomical structure. It's not something that you will see on an X-ray. Ego is an informational structure. That's what the term "ego" actually means: it is a Latinized translation of "das Ich," which is German for "the I." "The I" is "the information" that you have about you.

The ego-based view of the self is as unstable as a table on three legs. There are three issues with ego we need to examine, and they all start with the letter I. "The I" (ego) hinges on identification with impermanent information. Let's take a closer look.

Ego is information. Ego is a collection of self-descriptions, just a bunch of words written on the mirror of your consciousness. Let's say I point at the moon with my index finger. Is my finger the moon that I am pointing at? Of course not. Now ponder this: are you the information that you have about you, or are you that which this information is about? Are you a self-description or that which you are describing?

Ego is identification with the external. Identification is a process of pointing at something external, at something outside of you, and equating yourself with that. We've already touched on that concept earlier in the chapter. Identifying yourself with what you are not is absurd. Identifying yourself with something that you are not is like pointing one finger at yourself and the other finger at something else and then claiming that you are pointing at the same thing. The idea that you = this or that you = that is like shooting two arrows in two opposite directions and claiming that they are going to hit the same target.

Ego is impermanence of form. Self-esteem, self-worth, and self-view are various ego forms, various forms of information that we have about ourselves. Ego is information about our form, not about our essence. Forms change. "How" you are at any given point isn't fixed—it's in constant flux. When we identify with how we are, we are identifying with the fleeting, with the impermanent, with the transient. States of mind, states of mood, and modes of being are but ever-changing forms of you. The role you play, what somebody thinks about you, the thought you have about yourself, the number on your bathroom scale—all this is but information about you. When we identify with how we are, we identify with the transient. There is no permanence in that. This kind of identity is like writing on the surface of a pond. No matter how factual your self-description is, it dissolves just as it is being written.

sowing the seeds of lotus awareness

Having surveyed the limitations of the ego-based identity, let us now pause for some experiential prep work before we continue. It's time to sow the lotus seeds of awareness. You can read through the following exercises as meditations or work through them experientially. Following these exercises, we'll take one more look at ego-based identity before we wave our final goodbye. We will then preview lotus identity and talk about the specifics of how to cultivate it. In the meantime, roll up your experiential sleeves and get ready to plant.

plant a lotus seed:
clean slate, fresh start

Using a pencil (not a pen), draw a square with each side measuring about an inch. Let's call this paper square (no offense) "You." This square is the *tabula rasa* (the blank slate) of your consciousness. Now divide this square into four quadrants. In the first square, write down your bio-data (sex, age, race, weight, height). In the second square, write down your social data (job, relational status, employment status, political affiliation, gender, and so on). The third square is for writing down what you like (favorite color, movie, book, pastime). In the fourth square, write down what you dislike (what gets to you, your pet peeves, and so on). If the quadrants feel too small, don't worry about it; just cram it in, abbreviating if necessary. No need to be comprehensive; just jot down a few things for each category. Now, look at the drawing. What do you notice? A lot of ink, huh? That's right: "you" disappeared. First there was the tabula rasa of your consciousness, the clean slate of your essence. Then you divided it up into mental categories (bio-data, social data, likes, and dislikes). Then you filled in these cubicles of your mind with informational stuff. And as a result, you can now barely see you behind all this information!

Now, word by word, erase all this busy pencil work to restore the clean slate of your consciousness. Catch a glimpse of your essential self.

plant a lotus seed:
the mirror you

Now let me show you a tabula rasa. Find an erasable marker and a mirror. On the mirror, draw a square again measuring about an inch on each side. Let's call this mirror-square "You" (and this time I mean it as a compliment; it will become clear in a bit). Divide this square into four parts, as you did in the preceding exercise, then fill it in the same way as you did before.

Look at this square. The mirror you is eclipsed by the information. Now wipe the mirror clean. Meditate on how this applies to you. Recognize that the mirror doesn't cling to the information. Why should you?

---

plant a lotus seed:
the mirror of am-ness

Let's start over. Draw another square on the mirror. Write "I am" right above it. We'll assume that the entire surface of the mirror inside this square means "I am."

Divide the square into four quadrants. In the first section, write down your gender. In the second section, write down your relational status (single, married, partnered, engaged, or divorced). In the third section, write down your age. The fourth section is for your profession or job.

If you look at this mirror as a whole it reads, for example, "I am male, single, thirty-five, engineer" or "I am female, married, forty, English teacher." If you look at each quadrant, you get a different picture: each quadrant has its "I am male," "I am single," "I am thirty-five," "I am an engineer"; or, "I am female," "I am married," "I am forty," "I am an English teacher." When examined separately, each section presents a misleading picture. Each reads as an exhaustive description of who you are, and yet it is obviously incomplete. You aren't just your gender or your relational status or this or that. You aren't any of this information in particular; and, if you re-read how we set up this meditation, you'll realize that you're not even all of this information taken together. You are the mirror, not what's written on it—the mirror of am-ness, not the information on it. Wipe it clean!

plant a lotus seed:
space in between

Now let's try a variation. This time, find a large, wall-mounted mirror, preferably a full-length mirror. Draw a square again, but make it bigger this time. Write "I am" right above it. Divide the square into four sections and duplicate your responses from the preceding meditation: your gender, your relational status, your age, your profession.

Now, step back. What you see—metaphorically speaking—is a description of you. Remember that in the context of this exercise you are the mirror of am-ness and these words on the mirror are various descriptions of you. Recognize that there are many more ways in which you could and do describe yourself. So, let's do that.

Go ahead and extend the lines of the square to the very edges of the mirror, in all directions, so that the entire mirror is now divided into cubicles. What should you do with the phrase "I am"? Wipe it off: make room for self-description. Spend a few minutes writing various self-descriptions, writing one word per cubicle. Fill up the mirror.

Step back. Looks a little busy, huh? This is basically a picture of your self-concept, including the sort of informational luggage you carry with you at all times. This is your internal informational snapshot of who you are. Now recall how we set up this exercise. You are the mirror, not the words on it. You are the space in between all this mental ink. Clean it all off!

plant a lotus seed:
eclipsed by information

Let's start over. Position yourself in front of the largest mirror you have. Let's agree to call this entire mirror you. Let's agree that every bit of ink that comes out of the erasable marker in your hand is information about you.

While looking at the mirror, start shading it over with broad but dense strokes of the erasable marker. As you do this, notice your face begin to disappear behind the ink. Cover the entire mirror. Step back. Where are you? Your face has been eclipsed by the information about you. That's why you've lost sight of you. How can you see your true self if all you ever see is your self-descriptions? This book is about learning to clean your self of this informational dirt, about leveraging the capacity for self-cleaning. We'll explore this more later. For now, wipe the mirror off to once again see you.

plant a lotus seed: impermeability is invulnerability

We'll use different props this time: a cup of water, a hand-held mirror, and a sheet of paper. Put the mirror and the sheet of paper flat and side by side on a table or other surface. Sprinkle both with a few drops of water. Notice how the water beads up or pools on the surface of the mirror. Notice how the water penetrates the surface of the paper, soaking through.

Now pick up the hand-held mirror and turn it sideways. Let the water drip down. Put the mirror down. Pick up the sheet of paper and hang it sideways. Notice the difference. Whereas the mirror dried itself off in pretty much no time, the sheet of paper is still soaked and will remain soaked for quite some time.

So what's going on here? What accounts for the differences between these two surfaces? One is continuous and, thus, impenetrable and invulnerable (the mirror); the other is porous and, thus, absorbent, penetrable, and easily affected (the paper). The mirror is easy to dry; one wipe does it. Because of its absorbency, the paper has a much slower drying time. You could use another piece of paper to soak up some of the water from the first piece, but that first sheet will remain damp for a while. How come? The water has effectively entered the structure of the paper. Whereas the mirror's surface stood effective guard against invasion of the water, the paper allowed water to trespass and get inside. The water is no longer on the surface of the paper; it has been absorbed into the structure of the sheet. Even when the sheet of paper dries, it won't be the same. While the mirror, when dried, is the same as before, the paper is permanently damaged and warped.

What's my point with all this surface physics? Impermeability is invulnerability. Metaphorically speaking, the mirror of your consciousness is plastered with paper layers of self-narrative and self-descriptions. When you come in contact with the water of information, you get soaked through. But not all the way! This book is about helping you rediscover that self-cleaning, impermeable, immutable, invulnerable core self.

---

plant a lotus seed:
the wet book of ego

Gather the following: a credit card, a piece of paper, a pen, and a cup of water. Write your name on the piece of paper. Now, sprinkle some water on your name on the credit card and on your name that you have inked on the piece of paper. Notice what happens. While the ink of your name on the piece of paper begins to run and dissolve, your name on the plastic card remains intact. Let a few minutes pass. Wipe the credit card dry. Now try to soak up and dry up the water from the piece of paper. Your name on the credit card is completely unaffected. Your name on the piece of paper is damaged: a little smudged, diffused, somewhat dissolved.

The moral of the story? The transient doesn't last. Your name on the credit card is embossed and, as such, is part of the inalienable structure of the card. Your name on the piece of paper is written, added to the surface. Ego is information about us. It's added. First, we *are*. Then we seek reflection in a variety of informational mirrors. Finally, we internalize this information about us and confuse it with what is truly us, mistaking the words of self-description that we wrote down on the mirror of our am-ness with the mirror itself. Ego, in short, is an in-house logbook of self-descriptions, a collection of our favorite quotes about ourselves, a résumé of our accomplishments, and so on. Ego is an added self. As a result, it is vulnerable. A little character assassination does an easy wet job on our self-concept. A drop of disapproval, and the carefully crafted calligraphy of our identity begins to dissolve. Somebody calls us this or that enough times, and we forget our original built-in identity of name-less-ness.

the ego collects informational dirt

Let's summarize what we have established. Ego is porous, needy, perpetually incomplete. Full of holes, it fills up with informational dirt. Any time you seek approval and identity with others' thoughts about you, you trade an "I" for a "this" or a "that," a self for a not-self.

Ego is adhesive. It attaches. It clings. It identifies and bonds with the external. Ego wants evidence of its existence. In chasing the echo of its own presence, ego relies on reflection, validation, and approval from the outside. It becomes dependent on the reflection in the informational mirror, on compliments, on its status and rank. Ego clings to form. It uses form as evidence of its essence. "I am this," we think; "and this," we add; "and this," we add again—covering up our essence with layers of informational paint.

But since form is always changing, the attachment to form leads to ego wounds. Just as soon as you cast an anchor of identity in a given "here and now," just as soon as you get used to identifying yourself with "this" or "that," the world changes. The connection between what you are and the circumstance-specific description tenses up and snaps. Another adhesion (attachment) leads to another lesion (ego wound). Suddenly, you're cut off from the mirror. The familiar reflection is gone and so is the sense of identity. "What am I if I am no longer this or that?" we wonder in panic and rush to re-invent our selves. Needy and clingy, we shop for a perfect mirror that will show us the way we want to be seen, chasing another informational identity, another echo, another reflection, another attachment to the external. In this perpetual process of reaching out for an answer to the question about what and who we are, we accumulate informational dirt, as if drenched in glue. No wonder we get stuck.

Information-based (ego-based) identity is a life of dependence on the external. It is the path of gradual alienation from that essential sense of self, a superficial reliance on the form, on the description, on the reflection in the situational and social mirror. Ego—as a base of identity—is always outsourced. It doesn't belong to us. It is a collection of internalized trophies, strokes, compliments, approvals, and appraisals. It is an unsatisfying pocket full of crumbs. It has to be. Information-based identity lacks enduring essence. That's the fate of any form. Form always changes. And as such, even in the best-case scenario, it is only as firm as very wet sand.

Whereas ego clings, attaches, gets stuck, and accumulates informational dirt, lotus-like identity self-cleans, detaches, grows, and remains pure. Whereas ego-type identity references the external (one's status, circumstance, others' thoughts), lotus-like identity references only itself. Whereas ego-type identity is informational in nature, lotus-like identity is experiential in nature. Whereas ego-type identity is superficial and tenuous (based on form, on information), lotus-like identity is a deep and immutable identity: it is based on essence.

identity detox formula: dis-identify and re-identify

Cleaning is separation. Indeed, to clean is to separate dust from a desk, a splattered bug from a windshield, tomato sauce from a shirt. To detox your identity, you have to *dis-identify* (separate, detach, purify) *what you are not* from *what you are* and then re-identify with what you are. Thus, identity detox begins with dis-identification from the specific information about you (that misrepresents, mischaracterizes, misidentifies you), and it ends with re-identification, with a return to self.

It is important to not confuse dis-identification from information with detachment from or indifference to information. Dis-identification is not detachment. Dis-identification from information means that you know that you are not this or that information. Detachment is when you don't *care* about this or that information. It's entirely possible for you to dis-identify from the information about you and still care about the information and act upon it. It would be a mistake to think that by dis-identifying from the information about you, you should also ignore it. The next two exercises will help you get a better sense of what I mean.

plant a lotus seed:
mirror yourself

Affix a sticky note to your forehead and check out your reflection in the mirror. What do you see? A misrepresentation of your appearance. The mirror offers you information about an alteration to your appearance. Should you act upon this information? Should you make use of this visual feedback? Should you take this sticky note off at some point? Of course. Should you now re-think who you are and identify with the sticky note? Should you think of yourself as a sticky-note-person now? Should you modify your identity to be in line with your altered appearance? Of course not. Dis-identify from this information about your appearance (I am not this appearance, I am not this reflection of me) and use the information to restore your original look.

Now look at the mirror again. Say you see some evidence that you are overweight. Dis-identify from this information (I am not my weight, I am not my appearance) *and*, if it matters to you, act upon this information. Remember: dis-identification isn't detachment. No need to ignore facts—just ignore the illusion that you are the facts about you. You aren't.

The Criteria of Essential Self

The website "Exploring Chinese History" cites Candrakirti, a seventh-century Buddhist philosopher (who died around the time those 1,300-year-old lotus seeds were born) defining self as "an essence of things that does not depend on others [other things]; it is an intrinsic nature."[1] The question we still need to answer is this: what is self, and how shall we recognize it when we encounter it? I'd like to suggest the following two markers of real self.

Locality is the first criterion of the essential self. Experientially, subjectively, you are always *here* (wherever that "here" for you is), while the world is out *there*. To be yours, self would have to be located inside of you, not outside of you. Self is intrinsic (internal, inner, embedded). According to the Online Etymology Dictionary, the word "self" takes its linguistic root from the Proto-Indo-European word base *se,* which means "separate, apart."[2] The word "self" is kin to such *se*parating words as *se*gment, *se*ction, and *se*cret. Notice the "se" word base of all these terms. So, when I mention that self is inextricably linked to locality, it is this separateness I'm talking about. The word "self" is also kin (by way of *se*) to the word "several," which literally means those that are separate and thus diverse, multiple, different, and individual. It is this localized se-parateness, the apart-ness of self that assures its essential and indivisible individuality. (In chapter 6 we'll take another look at the issue of locality, separateness, and individuality as we discuss the possibility of a self-transcendent self.)

Permanence is the second criterion of the essential self. Indeed, any aspect of self that is impermanent, fleeting, and transient is by definition neither necessary nor sufficient for the existence of the essential self.

---

1 www.ibiblio.org/chinesehistory/contents/02cul/c04s03.html

2 www.etymonline.com/index.php?search=self&searchmode=none

plant a lotus seed:
no two are like one

Get two cups that look alike, and place them side by side. Recognize that as similar as they look, they are not identical. There are two ways to establish that. One method involves close examination and possibly complex measurement. The other involves plain common sense. Sure, you could weigh both cups on a highly sensitive scale to see that they are of different mass. You could examine the cups at very close range to see that there are numerous tiny differences between them. Or you could just recognize that since they are separate, they are inevitably not the same. Indeed, what immediately differentiates these two cups is that they have their separate coordinates in space. If these two cups were truly identical, if they were the same, they would share the same location in this world. In that case, there would be just one cup, not two.

Recognize that whatever is separate is fundamentally unique. Either cup exists independently of the other cup. Recognize that similarity isn't sameness. Sameness is a matter of locality, not a matter of comparison. Understand that it is exactly this principle of separateness that allows for the possibility of individuality and for the possibility of there being a separate self. Recall that both the words "separate" and "self" stem from the word base *se,* which means "separate." Recognize that if something exists separately from you, it is not you. See that if you can continue on, existing independently, without something else being a constant element of your existence, then that something is not you. Recognize that no two things or people are alike. If you are separate, you are beyond comparison.

plant a lotus seed:
essence is permanence

Fill a cup with water. Ponder whether this action changed the cup's essence. First, you had a cup. It existed independently of any water. It was separate from water. It was itself. Then you filled the cup with water. Did that change the essence of the cup? Not sure? Test it: empty the cup. Notice that it is wet. It was first dry; then, after it came in contact with water, it got wet. Ponder whether this has changed the cup's essence. Not sure? Do another test: let the cup dry out. Now the cup is exactly as it was.

Recognize that there is a certain kind of permanence to the cup's essence. The cup is not its contents. Ponder how this applies to you. Understand that you have a kind of essential permanence to you regardless of what you are preoccupied with (the contents of your life and the contents of your consciousness). Recognize that whatever you contain is just information about you—about what matters to you, about what your life is filled with, about what your head is full of. Can you see that all this is information and that you are not information? Conclude: *I am not my contents.*

plant a lotus seed:
essence isn't a coordinate

Get a cup and place it anywhere you like. Next, move the cup to a different place. Ask yourself: has the essence of the cup changed with a change of its location? Recognize that it has not. The cup exists in a space of its own. As long as this cup exists, it occupies a kind of movable space within the larger space of this world. The cup is an independent locality, a space unto itself that does not change. Appreciate that the essence of this cup, that which makes it itself, exists regardless of where you move its form. Recognize that essence is a kind of locality that is not a location. If you exist, you are what you are, wherever you are. Your location is information about where you are, and you are not the information about you. Conclude: *I am not my location.*

---

plant a lotus seed:
change in form is not change in essence

Get a cup you don't care for and chip it or scratch it. Ponder whether this chip or scratch has changed the essence of the cup. Recognize that a change in form is not a change in essence. Ponder: is there anything you could do to this cup's form to change its essence? Recognize that to answer this question you'd first have to establish what that essence is. Ask yourself: what is the essence of this cup? What makes this cup a cup? What is the inalienable characteristic of this cup? Would this cup be still this cup if you painted it over? Would this cup still be this cup if you broke it apart? Recognize the fundamental difference between essence and form. Recognize that the essence of this cup is its emptiness. Without it, it wouldn't be a cup. Recognize that as long as this cup is a cup (in other words, as long as you do not completely break it apart), its essence—its cup-ness—will remain intact no matter what you do to its form. Ponder how this relates to you. Recognize that as long as you are, you are going to be you, regardless of the form you take, regardless of the information that fills you, regardless of where you are. Celebrate this glimpse of your fundamental invulnerability! Conclude: *I am not my form.*

---

plant a lotus seed:
essence is a secret that cannot be told

Recall that the word "self" is related to the word "secret" by way of the Proto-Indo-European word base *se*, meaning "separate." Ask yourself: what is the secret of my essence? What is this that is only mine and cannot be communicated?

I'd tell you if I could. No one knows the secret of your essential self. And even though I can't define the secret of your essence, I'll try to describe it. You know you from not-you. That's right: only you can tell you from not-you. For me to be able to tell you from not-you, I'd have to *be* you, but I'm not. No one else is.

So, there it is—your lotus effect in a nutshell. Essential self knows itself: it knows itself by knowing what it is not. Recognize that while I'm able to describe your secret generically, I have no practical experience to do what you do. I wouldn't have a clue about distinguishing you from not-you. I have no experience being you. In fact, on some level, when I see you, I don't even see you—I see a not-me. If all I see is a not-me, if I never see you as you see yourself, then how could I ever learn to tell you from not-you? This "know-how" is the secret of your essence. Only you know it. And there's no way of explaining this know-how.

But just because you can't explain to someone else, just because you cannot tell someone else how you do it, that doesn't mean that you don't know. You do know the secret of your am-ness. As you look at the things around you, instantaneously you know that you are not this or that. As you look inside yourself and see various thoughts, feelings, and sensations pass through you, instantaneously you know: I am not this thought or that thought. So, keep asking yourself: what is the secret of my essence? How do I know me from not-me? Share it with yourself.

plant a lotus seed: I came upon myself

The following is an excerpt from Carl Jung's memoirs. Consider it a glimpse into someone else's budding lotus identity. See if you can relate to or recognize yourself in this.

I was taking the long road to school...when suddenly, for a single moment, I had the overwhelming impression of having just emerged from a dense cloud. I knew all at once: I am *myself.* It was as if a wall of mist were at my back, and behind that wall there was not yet an "I." But at this moment *I came upon myself.* Previously I had existed, too, but everything had merely happened to me. Now I knew: I am myself now, now I exist. Previously I had been willed to do this and that; now I willed. (1989, 89)

Willard Johnson, the author of *Riding the Ox Home: A History of Meditation from Shamanism to Science*, has this to say about Jung's experience, described above: "Jung...on the basis of such experiences, re-identified [his] ordinary 'I' consciousness with another spiritual selfhood....Though it took [him] many years to solidify...spiritual identity, it began in the initiatory experience of mystically ecstatic de-identification with the ordinary self" (1982, 190).

Ponder the meaning of what Jung is describing. Ask yourself: what is it that he discovered when he "came upon" himself?

conclusion: your lotus-identity preview

The lotus flower clings to nothing—not to mud, not to water, not to honey. Lotus-like identity is as unaffected by criticism as it is by compliment. Make no mistake: lotus-like self isn't oblivious to the external. Secure in its self-knowledge, it is unafraid to take the external input into account. It adapts to the change of circumstance as it needs to, even changing its form whenever necessary. But at all times it's in tune with its own essence, managing to remain fundamentally the same without selling out, without compromising its integrity, remaining self-congruent.

The mark of the lotus-type identity is the capacity to not take others' thoughts about you and reactions to you personally. A secure, lotus-like self understands that nothing is personal. Nothing can be personal. Whatever others say to you or think about you isn't really about *you*. After all, it's not the essential you that others actually have in mind; rather, it is their thoughts about the inessential, superficial, apparent, situational, circumstance-specific you. They are judging your form, not your essence. Your essence—by definition—is indescribable. Lotus-like self understands this and takes no offense. Lotus-like self never minds its own mind either. It recognizes that one's own mind is also nothing but a pond of informational mud, a stream of informational change, a never-ending succession of thoughts, feelings, and sensations that ultimately has nothing to do with one's essential self.

Lotus-like self is nonstick: information slides off of it, nothing wounds it, nothing rubs it the wrong way or strokes it the right way. It is its *own* way. Lotus-like, it grows wherever it grows, regardless of its informational circumstance, fundamentally unaltered and loyal only to its own essence. It rests in its primordial purity, self-referential, self-consistent, self-sustaining, self-maintaining, self-congruent, self-derived, self-reliant, self-sufficient, self-assured, self-identified, and self-same. It draws only one equation: "I am what I am. The rest is my form. I am not my form." It rolls in the slime of the circumstance and doesn't get dirty. It sleeps on the laurels of success and retains no flattering-but-fleeting scent. It accumulates no baggage of external descriptions. It exists outside language and is immune to mischaracterizations and false information about its form. It defends nothing; just explains, if necessary. It rolls with the resistance as if walking through an empty field. It doesn't bother to defend its transient external forms and manifestations, leaving it up to the river of life to edit and update the reality with new forms and new manifestations. Like the sacred lotus of Asian philosophy, the essential self simply grows, pursuing the arrow of its well-being through the muddy waters of life, without getting entangled in the underwater weeds, without getting carried away by language, without getting uprooted by the undertows of change. The lotus identity is the original face, not the informational personality mask on it. Cultivating this essential self sounds like a tall order, doesn't it? Worry not: you already have it. What's left is to detox this self from what it is not.

PART 2

dis-identify from what you are not

CHAPTER 3

neti it out

The Self is not this, not that, precisely because it is the pure Witness of this or that, and thus in all cases transcends any this and any that.

Ken Wilber

Once we become aware of what we are not, we begin to uncover and discover who and what we truly are.

Lama Surya Das

This human being is composed first of this external covering, the body; second, the finer body, consisting of mind, intellect, and egoism. Behind them is the real Self.

Vivekananda

Having sown the lotus seeds of insight, we are now ready to weed out the false identities that obscure your essential self. In this undertaking we will leave no identification unquestioned. We will mow through this field of misinformation about what we are with diamond-cutting mercilessness.

our three tools

We have three meditational tools at our disposal.

Criteria of essential self. Our first blade is the criteria we set for separating the grain of the essential self from the chaff of inessential information, the criteria of *locality* and *permanence* that are the two sides of one and the same coin of essence.

Neti-neti. Our second blade is an ancient informational sickle of "neti-neti." Neti-neti is an expression from Upanishads, an ancient Indian text. The term translates from Sanskrit as "not this, not this" (or "neither this nor that"). L. C. Beckett, in his book *Neti-Neti: Not This, Not That,* explains the neti-neti expression as "an expression of something inexpressible" (1959, 29). Beckett explains that the phrase neti-neti expresses the "suchness" (the essence) of that which it refers to when "no [other] definition applies to it" (1959, 92).

We will use the phrase neti-neti ("not this, not that") as a rapid analytical conclusion of what we are not. You will notice that the subtitles of the meditations that follow begin with the phrase "neti it out." By *neti it out*, I mean for you to dis-identify from this or that, to separate yourself from what you are not. When I call upon you to "neti it out," I am inviting you to recognize that *you are not a given this, you are not a given that.* The call to neti it out is a call for freedom, an encouragement to break away from any given mirror, to cut the umbilical cord of identification, to pull up the anchor of your identity and resume sailing the seas of your essence. "Neti it out!" is a call to self-clean, a call to detox.

Mindfulness. Our final tool is vipassana-style mindfulness. Unlike neti-neti, mindfulness is a process of passive dis-identification from information. But don't be fooled by the apparent gentleness of mindfulness as a dis-identification tool: it is a scorched-earth napalm-efficacy informational dissolvent.

Have no doubt about it: we will be cleaning the house of ego-self of all its toxic informational clutter. Our goal is 360-degree identity detox. By scraping off one layer of informational dirt at a time, we get closer and closer to what we are. Remember that, in this process, each identity we shed is not a loss but a gain of a degree of freedom. We are dumping the informational ballast, shedding falsehoods, cleaning house, fumigating the informational ghosts of our past, liberating essence from its informational form. In other words, lotus-like, we are growing our way to clarity. So, that's the mandate of this chapter.

Please note that the exercises below will combine the neti-it-out attitude with a "me/not-me" check. A typical exercise will first zoom in on a certain aspect of information that we tend to identify with. Following this, you will be offered an opportunity to cut the given anchor of identity (to neti it out) and to clean up the informational mess with a straightforward me/not-me check. Initially, we will be weeding out false identity with a blade in each hand. After the first set of exercises, I will be putting the me/not-me blade in your hand only now and then, when we're working with a particularly thorny identity issue. Toward the middle of this chapter, we will put the neti-neti blade and the me/not-me blade aside and get some weeding practice with the machete of mindfulness.

On another process note, let me point out that this is the largest chapter of the book for a reason. You might think of chapters 1 and 2 as college, and this chapter is the subsequent internship. I hope you approach it as such. I encourage you to not just read through this chapter but to experientially engage in all of its exercises. Take your time clearing out the weeds. After all, you are cultivating the garden of self! If, come your psychological spring, you want to see lotus blossoms, then roll up your sleeves and sweat a little. I'll see you on the other side of this endeavor, when, pleasantly exhausted and purified by the hard labor of identity detox, we will do a little stargazing as we look at what you really are.

props: mirror, marker, mind

Before we proceed, there are three items you need: a mirror, a marker, and your mind. You'll be needing the reflective benefit of the mirror to enable your capacity for self-reflection. At times you'll need a hand-held mirror (as a kind of reflective tablet to write on; you'll see what I mean in a moment). At other times, a full-sized mirror will be most useful. You'll also need an erasable marker. If you don't feel like messing with all that, a notepad and something to write with would do. But, ultimately, none of this is necessary. Everything I'm asking you to do in this chapter, you can do in your mind—that is, as long as it's open.

I'll be challenging the most seemingly self-evident constants of your self-definition. At times, you'll be convinced that I'm totally bonkers until what I am proposing finally clicks. So, for you to suc-cessfully complete this identity detox project, it's important that you keep an open mind and not weed me out prematurely. If what you're reading doesn't make sense to you, if you feel like your dis-identifica-tion sickle has hit a stone, then step aside and have a breather, trying a different exercise in the meantime. When you're ready, come back to finish the exercise that was giving you trouble. There's no rush. You have the rest of your life to figure out who and what you really are. I, myself, am just catching on!

ten mirrors of identity

In dis-identifying from what we are not, we will look into the follow-ing ten mirrors of identity:

1. The Mirror of Reflection (physical mirror)

2. The Mirror of Others' Minds, Approval, and Feedback (social mirror)

3. The Mirror of Circumstance, Status, Rank, and Reputation (situational mirror)

4. The Mirror of Roles, Membership, and Affiliations (relational mirror)

5. The Mirror of Action, Professional Identity, Performance, and Pastime (behavioral mirror)

6. The Mirror of Possessions and Ownership (material mirror)

7. The Mirror of Body, Age, and Health (bio-data mirror)

8. The Mirror of Time, Memory, and Imagination (temporal mirror)

9. The Mirror of Language, Words, and Description (linguistic mirror)

10. The Mirror of Consciousness (inner mirror)

The metaphor of the mirror is essential. Here's what Antonio T. de Nicolàs has to say on this point in his profound work *Four-Dimensional Man: Meditations Through the Rg Veda*:

> [L]ooking in the mirror is…one of the most important philosophical acts we perform on ourselves daily. To begin with, the mirror gives us only an image, and this is a triviality. However, the triviality may turn into a nightmare or a liberation the moment we start looking carefully (philosophically) at the image in the mirror, for the image we see in the mirror is always an image we recognize in relation to a very similar image we saw previously in the mirror; and this, in turn, we recognize in relation to another image we saw in the mirror—and so on. The fact that we lump all these images under the same personal pronoun "I" is trivial; for this "I" is, again, a linguistic image within a mirror of language that reflects whatever images we *decide* to conjure up. However,

the decision about which criteria to use in relating to these images is not in the images, in the mirror, but is entirely up to the language-user or mirror-user to decide. The mirror confronts us with these two possibilities; we may acknowledge the source of the images—namely, us, I, man, woman—as forever unknowable and unidentifiable, or we may reduce ourselves to the image in the mirror. Unfortunately, this second choice is the one we usually take;...by reducing ourselves to the image in the mirror, we have chosen to *live* in the mirror." (1976, 82)

The mirror teaches us about our own essence, about how to reflect without clinging. By looking at the mirror we learn how to do the same.

Breaking Away from the Physical Mirror: I Am Not a Reflection

In my opinion, there are three inventions that have fundamentally changed the trajectory of human civilization. The first one was the invention of fire keeping. Fire set us free. It bought us time to sit down and reflect. The second is the invention of the wheel. The wheel put us on the road. It kicked off progress and set us in motion. The wheel yanked us out of contemplation. The third is the invention of the mirror. The mirror gave us a chance to reflect on ourselves while still on the go. The mirror gave us an opportunity to return to introspection without slowing down the wheels of progress. But we misused the mirror: we have confused the reflection in the mirror with the one looking at it. As a result we got stuck in the mirror. We started to worship the false idol of reflection. It's time to break away from the mirror: you are not a reflection.

the meaning of a reflection

Neti it out: *I am not a reflection.*

Go to a mirror. See your reflection. Realize that what you're seeing isn't you. You are here, in front of the mirror. What you are looking at isn't you; rather, it's your reflection. There it is, a reflection of you, on the surface of the mirror. You are not that.

With an erasable marker, cross out, X-out your identification with the reflection in the mirror. Draw an X over your image in the mirror. Now, take another look at the reflection in the mirror: see not-you. Decisively write on the mirror: "I am not my reflection!" Add: "Void identification!" Free yourself from the mirror. Ponder the effect of this for a few minutes. Wipe out the mess.

Me/not-me check. Locality question: where is this information located, inside or outside of you? This reflection of you is located outside of you; it is on the surface of the mirror. Conclude: *since this information (reflection on the mirror) is outside of me, it is not me. I am not this reflection.*

the inaccuracy of reflection

Neti it out: *I am not a reflection. I am not a distortion.*

Take another look at your reflection in the mirror. Realize that although this image you see in the mirror looks like you, it's not you: similarity isn't sameness. You are three-dimensional. The image is two-dimensional. The mirror always shortchanges. Realize that any reflection is a distortion. Recognize: *I cannot be adequately mirrored.* Conclude: *I am not this distortion.* Decisively write on the mirror: "I am not a distortion!" Add: "Cancel identification with image!" Ponder this for a few minutes. Wipe out the mess.

Me/not-me check. Locality question: where is this information located, inside or outside of you? Outside of you. Conclude: *I am not this reflection.*

---

the mirror's inability to reflect the inner

Neti it out: *I am not what others see. I am not the outer/external.*

As you stand in front of the mirror, think, "I wonder if the mirror can reflect what I'm thinking?" Look at the mirror to see if you can see the reflection of this very thought as you are thinking this thought. Try another thought. Recognize that the mirror cannot read your mind. Remind yourself that no one can. Recognize: what I am inside is not transparent to others. With your erasable marker, write on the mirror: "I am not this outer!" Add: "End confusion! Inner ≠ outer!" Conclude: *I am not what others see. I am not my outer.*

Me/not-me check. Locality question: where is the information about your outer appearance located, inside or outside of you? Outside. Indeed, how others see you, their perception of you, is in their heads, which is outside of you. It's the same with the reflection in the mirror. The mirror with your reflection is outside of you; therefore, it's not you. Conclude: *I am not my outer appearance, or the reflections of it, or others' thoughts about it.*

---

test the sovereignty of your essence

Neti it out: *I am not a reflection.*
I am not dependent on the mirror.

Look at the mirror. See your reflection. Now move and notice the reflection move. Recognize that you have a hierarchical superiority over your reflection in the mirror. It depends on you, not you on it. Try stepping out of the line of reflection. Notice that the reflection disappears. Notice that you didn't. Here you still are, sovereign in your existence. Reflection or not, you exist. That's self-evident. Celebrate this independence of the reflection. Assert: *I am independent of the mirror.* Write on the mirror: "I don't depend on the mirror!" Add: "End dependence on the mirror!" Add: "Free of the mirror!" Wipe the mirror (and the mirror of your consciousness) clean. Conclude: *I am not a reflection.*

Me/not-me check. Locality question: where is this mirror located, inside or outside of you? Outside of you. Conclude: *I am not a reflection on this mirror, or this mirror, or any other mirror.*

---

no correspondence between the inner and the outer

Neti it out: *I am not the outer me.*
I am not what I see in the mirror.

Look in the mirror. Now look inside yourself (figuratively). Now look back in the mirror. Notice that there is no correspondence between what you see inside and what you see outside, in the mirror. Realize that there is no comparison between the inner you and the outer you. Write on the mirror: "This has nothing to do with the real me!" Add: "I am not in the mirror!" Ponder this for a few minutes. Reset! Conclude: *I am not my outer. I am not a reflection in the mirror.*

Me/not-me check. Locality question: where is this image of you located, inside or outside of you? This image of you is outside of you. Thus, you are not it! Conclude: *I am not this image in the mirror.*

---

weightlessness of the inessential

Neti it out: *I am not a reflection of my reflection in the mirror.*

Look at your reflection in the mirror. How much does it weigh? Recognize that the reflection is weightless. Ask: why do I give so much weight to this weightless reflection of my form in the mirror? Ask: how does this weightlessness pull me down so much? Ask: who gives this reflection the gravity of significance? Write on the mirror: "N/A" (for "not applicable"). Add: "This is a reflection of my form. A reflection of my form says nothing about my essence! A reflection of my appearance does not reflect my essence!" Ponder. Wipe away your writing. Conclude: *I am not a reflection of my reflection in the mirror. I am not my appearance.*

Me/not-me check. Locality question: where are you? On the surface of the mirror, in somebody's mind? No. You are not outside yourself. You are not a reflection on the mirror or a thought in someone's mind. All that is outside of you, and therefore is not you. Conclude: *I am not a reflection of others' thoughts or a reflection on the surface of the mirror.*

Breaking Away from the Social Mirror: I Am Not Others' Minds

When we aren't looking into physical mirrors, we seek reflection in the mirrors of others' minds. We frequently identify ourselves through others' thoughts. Others' thoughts about us become our thoughts about us. Others' conclusions about us become our conclusions about us. We soak up others' information about us like paper soaks up water, and we get warped in the process.

Wring out all this informational dirt of approval and disapproval that you've soaked up. Our goal here is to dis-identify from others' minds and to restore the sovereignty of your own self-appraisal.

mirror named Bob

Neti it out: *I am not what others think.*
I am not others' thoughts about me.

With an erasable marker, name the mirror "Bob." Look at Bob. Look at Bob looking at you. Realize that there is no difference between a mirror Bob and a real Bob. If mirror Bob were a real Bob, he wouldn't be seeing you, but a reflection of you distorted by the mirror of his mind. He would be seeing you through the subjective lens of his point of view. Realize that whether you're standing in front of Bob the mirror or Bob the human, you are not what either Bob "sees."

Now think of someone who you believe has unfavorable thoughts about you or unrealistic expectations of you. Write that person's name on the mirror. Recognize that this other mind doesn't see you the way you see yourself inside, the real you. He or she just sees you the way you reflect in the mirror—distorted, two-dimensional, all surface. Write the following on the mirror: "I am not others' minds! I am not what others think I am! I am not others' opinions or thoughts about me!" Get specific: write "I am not what so-and-so (insert the real person's name) thinks!" Walk away from the mirror of the other's mind. Let the mirror think whatever it wants to think. In a bit, erase the mirror's thoughts about you.

Me/not-me check. Locality question: where is the other's opinion of you located, inside or outside of you? Outside, of course. Thus, others' opinions of you, thoughts about you, and reaction to you are not you. Conclude: *I am not others' thoughts about me. I am not others' mind-forms about my essence.*

compliments don't complete me, criticisms don't diminish me

Neti it out: *I am not others' thoughts of approval or disapproval about me.*

Zhuangzi, an ancient Chinese Daoist, speaks of a sage: "If the whole world were to praise him he would not have been encouraged; if the whole world were to condemn him he would not have been deterred. He was steadfast about the difference between the internal and the external" (Tzu 2007, 85).

Ponder the meaning of the word "compliment." The word is related to the verb "to complete." But let me ask you this: what does a compliment complete? What happens when somebody observes that you are bright or good looking? It depends. If you are in doubt about your appearance or your intelligence, then a compliment seems to provide reassuring information. A compliment seems to plug the pores of the ego-self with informational putty. If, however, you have no holes, if you feel complete and monolithic in your self-view, a compliment has nothing to add. You can acknowledge the compliment out of politeness while, internally, knowing that it changes nothing about you. It's the same story with criticism, disapproval, or negative feedback. If you know the real you, you know that new information about you is just that—new information—and that you are not information. Practice repelling these extraneous opinions.

Stand in front of mirror Bob. On the mirror, with an erasable marker, draw a thought bubble that says "I like (insert your own name)." This is what Bob right now thinks about you. What you have here is a visual simulation of approval. Recognize that you are not somebody's thoughts of approval. Let mirror Bob be fond of you. Write the very compliments that you crave. Step back to recognize that you are not these compliments, these words of praise and approval. Recognize that nothing has fundamentally changed about you. See that if a real-life person was right now thinking favorable thoughts about you, it would not in any way add anything to your life. At best, if you knew that somebody was enamored of you, you'd have a favorable thought about yourself.

But what does your thought about somebody's thinking favorably of you add to you? If you're not sure, test it. Right now, have the thought: "Bob likes me..." Big deal! You know those endless circulars with coupons and the other unsolicited junk mail you get every day? Opinion is just like that: it's spam. You know those promo flyers people pass out on the street as you walk by? Subjective appraisal is just like that: it's an informational flyer without wings. It takes you nowhere objective. You might say: I thought I looked good today, and when they complimented me, I got a confirmation of what I had thought. No you didn't. An opinion cannot validate an opinion. Subjective doesn't translate into objective. Preferences can be tallied (a million people downloaded this or that song), but they cannot be rank-ordered (this aesthetic position, this taste, is *better* than that aesthetic position, that taste).

Now, let's change Bob's mind with a new thought bubble: "I don't like (fill in your name)." Ponder the change. Bob's mind has been changed—but you haven't. Regardless of what Bob is thinking, you are still you. Recognize that you are not others' thoughts about you. Write on the mirror: "I am not others' likes or dislikes!" Add: "I am not others' thoughts of approval or disapproval!" Write on the mirror: "There is an unchanging part of me, a part of me that always remains the same, whether I am liked or disliked." Write: "I am neither enhanced nor deflated by external information!" Meditate on this. Recognize that others' minds are outside of you. Thus, you are not others' thoughts—be they critical or flattering. Decisively wipe out identification with others' thoughts about you. Conclude: *I am not what others think, like, or prefer. I am not this external, subjective information about me. I am not this person's thought of approval or disapproval.*

Me/not-me check. Locality question: where are you? Are you outside, in others' minds? Or are you inside your own mind, wherever you are? Inside. Even when you are in others' thoughts (on others' minds), you are still physically outside of these minds, anatomically sovereign and physically independent from others' opinions of you. All that information is in the world, outside of you, and therefore is not you. Conclude: *I am not the information about me that is outside of me. I am not others' minds. I am not others' thoughts or opinions or feelings or attitudes about me.*

---

compliment the mirror

Neti it out: *I am not others' reflections on me.*

Write your impressions of the mirror in front of you. Note if you like its size, framing, or shape. Decide if you like this particular mirror or not. If you like it, write (with erasable marker) "Good mirror!" If you don't like it, write "Bad mirror!" Now change your mind: if you liked it before, wipe off "Good mirror" and write "Bad mirror" instead. If you didn't like it initially, wipe off "Bad mirror" and write "Good mirror" instead. Check to see if the mirror has changed. It hasn't.

Just like you cannot change the mirror with your opinons about it, others' reflections (thoughts or opinions) about you cannot change you. Look in the mirror and imagine that you are somebody else looking at you. Let the reflection in the mirror represent you for a few moments. Think: "Bad person!" or "Good person!" Check to see if the mirror changed. Recognize that, like a mirror, you don't change with the change of reflection. Ponder this and, lotus-like, wipe the mirror of your consciousness clean. Recognize: others' opinions of you reflect on them; others' opinions of you reflect on their values, tastes, preferences, biases, and expectations—not on you. Conclude: *I am not others' reflections on me.*

Me/not-me check. Locality question: where is this information located, inside or outside of you? Recognize that others' fleeting, changing opinions of you are physically outside of you. Permanence question: are you this fleeting, changing external information about you? Of course not. You are not this external, subjective flow of information about you. Conclude: *I am not others' fleeting, transient, impermanent thoughts, opinions, feelings, or attitudes about me. I am not others' flow of subjectivity.*

informational echo

Neti it out: *I am not what others think
about what others think about me.*

Get a hand-held mirror. Now position yourself with your back to a wall-mounted mirror and, holding the hand-held mirror to your side with its reflective surface toward the mirror behind your back, look at the mirror in your hand. What you see is a reflection of a reflection of you. A reflection of a reflection is an informational echo: the reflection from one mirror bounces off another mirror just like sound jumping from one cliff to another in the Grand Canyon.

This is a metaphor for gossip, reputation, notoriety, or fame. Remember, there is you and there are others. Others have thoughts about you and share them with each other. As this information is passed, others' minds change but nothing fundamentally changes about you. You are not information about you, nor are you the information about that information. You are not an informational echo. Conclude: *I am not others' thoughts about others' thoughts about me! I am not gossip, fame, or reputation!*

Me/not-me check. Locality question: where is gossip? Where is reputation? Where is fame? In others' minds, outside of you. Realize that you are not what is said, written, or thought about you. Shrug off the informational echo.

zero impact

Neti it out: *I am not the difference that*
I make. I am not others' reactions.

Get a pebble or a stone or some small but weighty object. Fill up your bathtub or your sink. Toss the stone into this body of water. Notice the impact, the splash, the ripples. Now fish out the stone, dry it off, and toss it onto the floor. Notice the lack of impact: no splash, no waves. Next, answer this: does the stone have an impact or not? Does it make a difference or not?

Recognize that while the impact provides information about a collision of variables, it does not say anything in particular about the variables themselves. Whether you have impact on others or not, whether this impact is favorable or unfavorable, impact has no effect on your essence. Whether a stone falls into a water-filled kitchen sink or onto the kitchen floor, it remains fundamentally the same—a stone. Sure, it can get banged up in the process, but that's not the issue. The issue is that the stone isn't the impact that it makes.

Let's say that you read this exercise and e-mail me saying that it made no impact on you. Should I conclude that I am a failure? Let's posit that I do. But as soon as I do, somebody else e-mails me to say that this exercise had a great impact on them. Should I then revise my view of self and conclude that I am a success?

Your impact on the world or lack thereof produces information about the interplay between you—the stone—and the particular surface with which you collide. Conclude: *I am not the effect I have on people. I am not others' reactions to me. I am not the impact I make.*

dynamics of subjectivity and resolution

Neti it out: *I am not a stereotype.*
I am not others' arbitrary opinions.

Historically, water was the original mirror. But being dynamic, water had no surface regularity in which to offer a consistent reflection. Let's learn from that.

Get a large skillet or a cookie sheet and place it on the kitchen counter. Fill it with water and wait for the water to settle. Now look down into this liquid mirror to see the reflection of your face. Get really close to the surface of this mirror, face to face with your reflection. Notice: your breathing affects the reflecting surface. Or maybe a strand of your hair falls right into the plane of reflection. Maybe, as you position your hands on each side of the counter to stabilize yourself, you will send a shiver of ripples along the water's surface.

Ponder what is going on here. Your very presence affects the mirror's ability to provide an accurate reflection. You have a direct, moment-to-moment influence on the mirror's accuracy. Get too close and this liquid mirror warps. But as you get farther away, the reflection loses resolution. Indeed, from a distance you don't see all the details. But when you get close enough to see your eyelashes, the mirror warps and distorts.

The liquid mirror teaches us about the dynamics of feedback. When you search for feedback from somebody you know, from somebody you are close to, you are looking into a warped mirror. The dynamics between the two of you have an effect on the accuracy of reflection. By being too close to this human mirror, you affect the very surface that you're looking into for feedback. Say that you ask your friend for feedback. You want to look into the mirror of her mind to learn about yourself. But your very request immediately threatens the status quo of your relationship. Your friend understandably wonders about how her feedback about you will affect the relationship. She, too, is looking into the mirror of your mind to see how what she says will reflect on her. As a result, she pulls her punches, sugar-coats, or says too little. Or she says too much. And there you are, in a feedback loop of two reflections, exchanging distortions rather than feedback.

If you choose to look for feedback from somebody you barely know, you end up with a reflection of very low resolution. It's like looking at a mirror from too great a distance. You see something but it's not clear what. The reflection is just not detailed enough. It's too generic. From a far enough distance, a reflection could be anyone's. Step far enough back from the mirror and all you see is an indeterminate, shadowy figure. It's a catch-22. If you want to see more details, you have to get closer; but getting closer reduces the objectivity of the reflection. If you want objectivity, you have to move away from the mirror, but then you lose out on the resolution of details. And so it is.

Conclude: *I cannot be adequately mirrored.* Reiterate to yourself: *I am not that distorted reflection in the mirror of somebody's mind.* Reiterate: *I am not that uninformative, low-grade, low-resolution, stereotype of a reflection in the mind of somebody who doesn't know me.* On the mirror, write: "I am not a stereotype! I am not a bunch of arbitrary opinions generated by others' minds!" On the mirror, write some stereotypes that others might have of you. Step back. Notice you as you separate from all this distortion.

Me/not-me check. Locality question: If you wanted to locate your stereotype, where would you find it? Outside: in somebody else's mind, in some piece of written communication, maybe in some kind of informal profiling guideline that is being passed as gossip. You would find it in the information outside of you. Conclude: *I am not others' sweeping generalizations about me. I am not a low-resolution snapshot in somebody's mind.*

you are not an affiliation

Neti it out: *I am not a Buddhist*
(or insert another affiliation that applies).

Chogyal Namkhai Norbu, a Dzogchen Buddhism teacher, says: "It makes no difference whether one considers oneself to be Buddhist or not. Basically, feeling oneself to be a follower of something or other is just a limit" (1996, 120). Indeed, any affiliation distracts us from our essence. You are not whom you are with. You are not whom you worship with. You are not your meditation practice. You are not your sports team. You are not whom you know. You are not your connections or your contacts list. So take a look in the mirror. Ask: who is reflected in it? Do you see a reflection of a Buddhist or of a Christian or of an atheist? Do you see a reflection of a fan of the Yankees or the Steelers? Really? As personally important as all these associations are to you, recognize that—in your essence—you are not any of these associations. You are not whom you are with. You are not a reflection in the social mirror. Conclude: *I am not my affiliations. I am not whom I hang out with, pray with, meditate with, go to school with, or go to war with. I am not my associations.*

Me/not-me check. Locality question: where is your sports team? Outside of you. Where's the crew you run with? Outside of you. Permanence check: were you you before you became a member of a country club? Yes. Will you still be you if you were to lose your membership? Yes. Recognize: you are not your time-specific, circumstance-specific memberships, affiliations, or connections. Conclude: *I am not my social ties.*

your personal hall of mirrors

Neti it out: *I am not what others think.*

Write on the mirror the names of *all* the people whose opinion of you matters to you (personally, professionally, or socially). Next to each name, write what you think they think you are ("good person," "bad person," "son," "worker," "genius," "slacker," "perfectionist," "neurotic," "smart," "confused," "too rigid," and so on). Step back and take a look. So, here you are, and there are a range of perspectives on what you are. No amount of information about you in others' minds equals you. You are not the information about you. You are not your press release, your Wikipedia entry, your face on a billboard, or the public opinion about you. Conclude: *I am not others' thoughts even if those thoughts are accurate.* Clean the mirror to shrug off this informational portrait of you in others' minds.

clean up the reflection

Neti it out: *I am not others' thoughts about what I was.*

Put an adhesive bandage on your forehead and look at your reflection. Now, without taking the bandage off, go to the mirror and try to remove the bandage *from the surface of the reflection.*

Realize that once another person has formed an image of you, he might be stuck with seeing that outdated reflection of you in the mirror of his mind. Understand that anyone's image of you is based on an outdated stereotype. Recognize that other people are looking at an outdated reflection of you in the mirror of their own consciousness. After all, in the time it takes for the reflected light to travel from your face to the mirror and from the mirror to the viewer's eyes and be comprehended as an image of your face, your face has already changed—it is already a fraction of a second older; your expression may even be different. Recognize that any reflection is a reflection of what was, not what is. We'll come back to this when we look in the mirror of time. In the meantime, conclude: *I am not a reflection of my past. I am not others' thoughts about what I was. I am not others' memories. I am not a stereotype.* Step back. Ponder. Clean off the inaccuracies.

Me/not-me check. Locality question: where is this information about you located, inside or outside of you? Outside of you. Conclude: *I am not an informational echo in others' minds. I am not a memory in someone's mind.*

---

realize that public opinion is a funhouse

Neti it out: *I am not consensus. I am not public opinion.*

Go to (or just imagine) a funhouse that features an array of distorted mirrors. Look around. What you see is the equivalent of public opinion about who and what you are. Every mind is a mirror. The subjectivity of each mind is the source of its distortions. Some minds will amplify what they consider to be your good traits; others will diminish them. Just as the warp of the funhouse mirror is responsible for the distortion of your image, so is the bias of a given mind.

Move around in front of these warped mirrors. Notice the distorted feedback. Smile in front of a convex mirror and see a grotesquely exaggerated reflection of your smile. Smile in front of a concave mirror and see the image of your smile focus into a pouty point. Imagine standing in front of a row of concave mirrors and seeing the image of your smile reduced to many pouty points. The consensus of these distorted reflections would not change the fact of their reflective error. Conclude: *I am not that* (the public opinion about you, even if it is in consensus). Write on the mirror: "Subjectivity + Subjectivity ≠ Objectivity." Write: "Ten same opinions don't add up to one objective truth!" Ponder. Erase your identification with the external.

turn a friend into a mirror

Neti it out: *I am not what others think.*

Ask a friend to sit silently across from you. Have them think some kind of thought about you. Realize that you are not the thought about you inside your friend's mind. Reiterate to yourself: *I am not another's thoughts.* Relax. Smile. Tune in to your invulnerability. Remember your secret: only you know the real you.

Me/not-me check. Locality question: where is your friend's thought? In your friend's mind (outside of you). You are not what's outside of you. Reiterate to yourself: *I am not others' mind forms (such as thoughts, feelings, sensations, opinions, or memories). I am not the information that others have about me in their minds.*

expect a discrepancy

Neti it out: *I am not others' expectations.*
I am not others' preferences.

Have a friend or an acquaintance expect something of you, in person or over the phone. Let her verbalize what she thinks or expects. Recognize the inevitable discrepancy between what others expect of you and what you are. Recognize that you are entitled to be exactly as you are. It's your life, after all! Conclude: *I am not others' expectations of me.*

Me/not-me check. Locality question: where is the discrepancy between others' expectations of you and you? In the form of a thought, in the mind of whoever is having this expectation of you (outside of you). Conclude: *I am not others' fantasies about what I should be. I am not others' failure of acceptance of what I am at any given point in time. I am not others' denial of my reality. I am not what's in others' minds.*

break the mirror of dependence

Neti it out: *I am not what others think.*

Get a cheap hand-held mirror and a hammer. Put some newspapers on the floor. Look into your mirror. See your reflection. Now place the mirror on the newspaper and gently bust it up. Break the reflection. Recognize that you remain unaffected. Think: "I am not the shards of my reflection. I am not the fragmented view that others have of me." Recognize that when others' view of you is shattered, just like this mirror, they no longer have a holistic view of you. They get stuck on this one thing you said, on this one act you did, and they lose sight of the rest of you (not that they ever had the real, comprehensive, exhaustive view of you anyway). A loss of a reflection doesn't have to be a loss of self. Conclude: *I am not the reflection that I lost.*

Me/not-me check. Locality question: where is the approval that you lost? Outside of you; therefore, it's not you. Where is so-and-so's limited perspective on what you are? In so-and-so's mind (outside of you). Conclude: *I am not others' new opinions of me just like I wasn't what they used to think of me. I am not what's in others' minds.*

Breaking Away from the Mirror of Action: I Am Not What I Do

If you are like most people, you tend to identify with what you do. It's rather Zen of you (but only when you're actually doing it). If you're a driver, then drive when you drive. If you are a cook, then cook when you cook. If you are a doctor, then doctor when you doctor. Be the action when you are in the process of the action. But once you're done doing what you are doing, be you.

consciousness comes without titles

Neti it out: *You are not your job.*

When you picked up this book and saw my credentials you may have thought, "This guy must know what he's talking about—he's a psychologist." If so, allow me to promptly disabuse you of at least one erroneous assumption you made. I am not a psychologist. Psychology is what I do (part of the time; right now, for example, I am doing something entirely different—I am typing that I'm typing). You are not what you do. You are not your actions. Rethink this identification with the behavioral. Edit your small-talk defaults: instead of saying that you are such and such (job), say that you *do* such and such job. Conclude: *I am not what I do. I am not my actions. I am not my job. I am not my career. I am not my profession. I am not my title. I am not my credentials.*

Me/not-me check. Permanence question: is any given behavior of yours a permanent part of you? No: you are reading now, but in a moment you might get up and do something else. Is your professional circumstance an all-encompassing behavioral description of you? No: today you are employed, tomorrow you may be collecting unemployment. You are not this ebb and flow of professional activity. Conclude: *I am not time-specific, fleeting information about what I do. I am not my behavioral signature. I am not the fleeting information about me that is subject to change.*

shedding work/service/ education identity

Neti it out: *I am not my work identity.*

If you're like most people, you will spend about a third of your adult life working for somebody. Employment is most likely a huge part of your identity and a source of meaning in your life. The loss of work identity that comes with being laid off, being fired, or even retiring can feel crushing. A good way to defend against that is to begin to dis-identify from your work identity while you still have it.

Naturally, this is a private process. I'm not calling on you to demonstratively burn your employee name tag in front of the main office. I am inviting you to take off your name tag psychologically. How? First of all, let's face it: no one is irreplaceable. If your job can survive without you, you can survive without your job. Second, resist corporate categorization and objectification of what you are, however well-intentioned it might be. Second, as flattering as it might feel to be an asset to your company, recognize that you aren't just a "human resource"; you are, first and foremost, a human being—not a sales force, but a life force. Third, dis-identify with your title: you aren't a regional manager, an executive assistant, a VP, or any other designation—you are you. You were you before this title, you are you now, and you will be you after this title. Title identification is especially pervasive in the military and law enforcement. Recognize that you are not your rank. Rank is information. You are not information. The education industry is another big identification player. You aren't the school you are in or went to. Your identity isn't at stake when your college sports team loses. Sure, networking on the basis of your college affiliation can provide career opportunities. But what does that "graduate of" lettering on your car's window really say about you? That you went to such-and-such higher education institution? Resist institutionalization.

With your erasable marker, list all of these professional and educational identifications, line by line. Use the "I = such-and-such" form. Then look at all this information. Is it important? Yes. Is it essential to your existence? No. Decisively strike through all these identifications with a marker ("I ≠ such-and-such"), one after another. Dare to conclude: *I am not whom I work for. I am not my job. I am not my rank.*

Me/not-me check. Permanence question: are you your title, your credentials, your rank? Maybe sometimes—five days a week from nine to five. But what about when you're asleep? Are you still a lieutenant or a CEO or a medic or a coach while you snore all tucked in under the covers? Of course not. Wake up from this informational dream to conclude: *I am not my professional garb; I am not my uniform. I am not my informational disguise.*

there is no "I" in the outcome

Neti it out: *I am not an outcome of what I do.*

Daisetz Suzuki, in his foreword to the 1953 classic Zen in the Art of Archery by Eugen Herrigel, offers a thought of dis-identification from the outcome of one's performance:

> "[t]he archer ceases to be conscious of himself as the one who is engaged in hitting the bull's-eye which confronts him."

The arrow is the extension of your arm. The arm is the extension of your body. The body is the extension of your mind. Your mind is the extension of the arrow of your consciousness. When you release the bowstring of your performance and when the arrow hits or misses the target, you are still standing where you were standing; you are still you, regardless of the outcome. You were there before any given outcome, and you will be there after a given outcome. But this outcome came out of you. It would not have happened without you. Remember: you are not the outcome of the outcome; it's the outcome that is the outcome of you. You are not your performance, you are the one who performs. Conclude: *I am not the outcome of what I do. I am not the outcome of my performance.*

Breaking Away from the Situational Mirror: I Am Not My Context

We often seek identity in our circumstance. The word "circumstance" stems from the Latin preposition *circum*, which means "around," and the verb *stare*, which means "to stand" (www.etymonline.com). A circumstance is that which stands around you, your surroundings, your context. Look around you for a moment. Notice what's around you. Perhaps you're in your living room with this book on your lap, a cup of tea at your side. Or maybe you are in bed with this book atop a blanket that rests atop your stomach, with your cat (or dog, partner, or spouse) snuggled up nearby. Or maybe you're in a late-night, near-empty subway car reading this book on a Kindle, sitting next to a snoring drunk.

No matter where you are, remember that you are not this physical context—you are that which it surrounds. That's obvious. What's less obvious is that you are not your cultural, ethnic, sociological, or racial circumstance either. Whatever your situational context, you are not your situation.

---

culture of one

Neti it out: *You are not your social status.*

As long as there are individuals, there will be individual differences. As long as there are individual differences, there will be differences in social and economic power. As long as there are socio-economic differences, there will be groupings and clusterings of these differences. And as long as there are groupings and clusterings of socio-economic differences, there will be social classes. To sum up, as long as there are individuals, there will be classes of individuals. There are no classless societies, but there are people who don't stereotype themselves.

You are not your birth circumstance. You are not your class, not your caste, not your social strata. These categories are simply information about your social standing. But you aren't where you stand. You aren't a cultural or sociological coordinate. A king isn't a king, a queen isn't a queen, an aristocrat isn't an aristocrat, a slave isn't a slave, an untouchable isn't an untouchable. You aren't old money. You aren't new money. You aren't a scion. You aren't a welfare mom. This is all background. You are the figure in front of it. You aren't the group, you are an individual. Group identification is informational bondage. Group identity turns the unique into a cliché.

Why not emancipate yourself from the informational ball and chain of social typecasting? Break the chains of group identification. Write on a mirror whatever social construction that you identify yourself with, using the "I = such-and-such" form. Use as many lines as you need to identify yourself. Now close your eyes, look inside, and notice you. Open your eyes: see the difference.

Decisively cross out all these identifications using the "I ≠ such-and-such" form, one after another. Wipe the mirror clean of all this self-stereotyping. Walk away. Conclude: *I am not my caste, class, clique, social rank, or social standing. I am not a socio-economic cliché. I am not a cultural stereotype.*

---

renew your origins

Neti it out: *I am not a product of my environment.*

You may think, "I am a product of my environment." You aren't. But this issue is a little trickier than mere dis-identification. After all, dismissing cause-and-effect and determinism of the past is no easy matter. But let's see if we can still do it on the fly.

The usual way of thinking about these matters is that you are either free (that is, you are not a product of your environment and your past) or not free (your path is determined by your environment and your history). However, the situation isn't really this black and white. Theoretically, we are free. But we aren't always operationally free. If you are mindless, you are on autopilot and your past determines your present. Mindlessness stands in the way of freedom. So, if you are sailing through life on autopilot, then, yes, you are a product of your environment. If, however, you are mindful, then in that moment of mindfulness you can make a free choice, a choice that is independent of your previous choices. In other words, by being mindful you stand to override your cultural conditioning, your historical programming, your autopilot. So, it's not a matter of free will versus determinism. You are both free and not free, depending on whether you are mindful or mindless. If you are mindless at any given point, then, in that moment, you are a product of your past, a product of your environment. If you manage to wake up, if you turn your mind on, then you stop being a product of your past. When mindless, you re-act; that is, you re-enact a previous course of action. When mindful, you act anew—you freely choose an original course of action. It is from this perspective that I call on you to recognize that you are not a product of your environment.

Here's an exercise to try to clarify this point. Clench your fist. Open it. Clench it again. Open it again. Clench it again. Open it again. Clench it and open it five more times. Now, clench it one more time...and *choose how* you open it. See the difference? First, your hand and your mind were a product of your past, both on autopilot as you kept opening your fist without consciously choosing how to open it. But when you woke yourself up, when you turned your mind on, you let go of your conditioning and exercised your free will. Instead of your present being willed by your past, *you*—not your past—willed your present. So, gather up this idea of being a product of your environment and a product of your past and clench it tightly into your fist. Feel the tension of this idea, feel the muscle-constraint of it and the mind-constraint of it, and...*choose* to open this fist of determinism and let it go. Recognize that you are not your origins. Renew your origins with a conscious choice to remain original. Conclude: *I am not a product of my past. I am not a product of my environment.*

Me/not-me check. Permanence question: are you what you chose to eat for breakfast yesterday? No. Are you some other choice from the past? No. Locality question: where is your upbringing? It's in the behaviors of your role models (outside of you). Where's the environment you grew up in? Somewhere on this planet, in some neighborhood, in some space-time coordinate outside of you that you call "back home" or "my past." Conclude: *I am not my past choices. I am not my informational roots. I am not my origins. I am not my informational circumstance.*

Breaking Away from the Mirror of Time: Not My Past, Not My Future

Self-description is a snapshot of how you are at a given point in time. The problem with describing yourself is that it takes time for us to describe whatever it is that we are describing. No matter how brief, there is an inevitable lapse between witnessing a moment of reality and then capturing it through a description. Consider this: by the time you conclude that you are "this," you are no longer the you that you began to describe. The river of life doesn't wait. The very moment you realized you had turned twenty-one, you were twenty-one plus a millisecond. So, time, too, fails us as a mirror.

---

mirror of the past

Neti it out: *I am not what I was.*

Look at the reflection of your face in the mirror. Right now you are seeing what your face looked like, not what it looks like right now. Indeed, your face is a breathing, living surface. It's not fixed. It's in constant flux. If you looked closely enough at it, say, with the help of time-lapse photography, you'd see the fuzz on your cheeks sprout up like grass, pores opening up and closing, and so on and so forth. So, when you look at your face's reflection in the mirror, what you see is what your face looked like a nanosecond ago.

Even reflection is a process. It's not outside of time. Fast as it is, it's not instantaneous. It takes time for light to bounce off your face and then off the mirror and then back to you for your eyes to see it and for your mind's eye to see what your physical eyes have seen. Sure, the physics of this and the neuro-info-processing involved in all this is fast. But there is nevertheless a *phase delay*.

So, take another look in the mirror of the past: it never shows you the present. Realize that you are never seeing your reflection in real time. Sure, the difference between you a nanosecond ago and you now is negligible. But I believe that as you play with this idea, the significance of the realization will be overwhelming. Now, if this was a one-time distortion, I can see how we could overlook that. But this is all you ever see when you look into the mirror. No mirror—physical or metaphorical—ever shows you what is in real time.

Write on the mirror: "I am not what I was." Recognize that you are what you are now, not what you were in your past. Add to the mirror: "This is my visual echo." Let this idea sink in. Wipe the mirror clean. Walk away to your real-time self. Conclude: *I am not a reflection of my past.*

Me/not-me check. Permanence/locality question: where is the you that you were yesterday? Nowhere. Recognize that the you you were no longer is. You, now, aren't what you were yesterday morning or even this morning. That you is nowhere to be found.

Put this book aside and go get the you that you were a moment ago. Let me look at both of you as the two of you (the you you were and the you you are) stand side by side. Catching my drift? You've changed. The new you irreversibly displaced and replaced the you that you were. There is no other you but the one reading this sentence right now. What remains of the old you is information: others' memories, old photos, a progress note in your therapist's file from the last time you went in for a session. You aren't that external, outdated, subjective information about you. Conclude: *I am not a ghost of the past.*

self is a memory lane

Neti it out: *I am not my memories.*

Spend an evening browsing through your photo albums. Look at a nice photo of yourself. Realize that it's actually not a picture of you, but a document of your past. Recognize that you are not your past. Recognize that there is no past at this moment. There is just this. Just this moment. This now. This you. Ilchi Lee, a Korean meditation teacher, says: "When we recognize that the past is only information, we will have taken our first step towards freeing ourselves from it" (2005, 142). Repeat this thought process with each and every photo that catches your eye. Conclude: *I am not what I was. I am not my memories. I am not the facts that I remember. I am not information about what was. I am not my past. I am not a memory of myself.*

review your résumé

Neti it out: *I am not my narrative. I am not my story.*

We tend to over-identify with our narratives. We get stuck in the character arcs of our own storytelling. Pull out your résumé. Recall how you built this story of your academic and professional life a line at a time. Recall how you'd save it on your computer and, when moving on (academically or professionally), you'd re-open it, edit it, and add to it. Realize that you've been writing the narrative of your life moment by moment. Realize that your narrative is still being written, that the story of your life will not be complete until the very last moment, until that moment that won't have the narrator to capture it.

Print out a copy of your résumé. Tear it up and *resume* the flow of your indescribable continuity. Recognize that you are not your story, you are the protagonist. You are not the narrative, you are the narrator. You are not the message, you are the messenger. Conclude:

I am no single moment. I am not a story, even if it's my story. I am not a narrative, even if it's my narrative.

Me/not-me check. Permanence question: are you at this very moment learning your ABCs or falling off your bicycle as you try to learn to ride it? No. Are you right now having your first kiss? Probably not. These moments, as real as they once were, have nothing to do with you right now. What does? This moment...and now, a moment later. Have you noticed how your self-description is always a moment too late? Conclude: *I am not my time shadow.*

---

let bygones be bygones

Neti it out: *I am not my accomplishments.*

Self is a memory of what you were. As such, self, with all its accomplishments and their implications, is a bygone. Let bygones be bygones. The informational self is a train of a wedding dress of a wedding that is already over. You kissed the reality. It kissed you back. Now, forget this glorious highlight of an accomplishment. Yes, you had your shining moment or two. Maybe hundreds. What now? It's time to plug back in to the reality that's still awaiting your attention, time to cut the anchor of accomplishments. Out of the long shadows of the past, it's time to bask in the sun that still shines.

You see, accomplishments, by definition, are in the past. You are not. Therefore, you cannot be your accomplishments. When we define ourselves through our accomplishments we are defining who and what we are now through the memories of the past. Look at your trophies, at your certificates of achievement, at your medals. You are not the house you built. You aren't the child you gave birth to. You aren't the life you saved. You are none of that. You are this life, right now. You are the real-time you, the you that you are *yet* to describe, the you that is always in progress. Realize that you are not your past behaviors and accomplishments or current thoughts (memories) of those behaviors and accomplishments. Conclude: *I am not my accomplishments. I am not my past glory.*

Me/not-me check. Permanence question: let's say that you developed a case of amnesia and forgot all you know about yourself. Would you still exist? Of course. You'd be confused as hell, but you'd still feel like eating if you felt hungry and peeing if your bladder got full. Understand: whatever autobiographical information about yourself that you've packed away for the future, you could do without it. Sure, if you lost all that information, you'd feel lost, but you wouldn't disappear. You'd take another breath and go on. If so, if you could exist without all that informational luggage, then how can it be an essential part of you? Conclude: *I am not my informational luggage.*

---

po

Neti it out: *I am not my potential. I am not my future.*

Edward de Bono, a paradigm-shifting thinker, introduced a verbal device designed to provoke original ("lateral") thought processes. This word is "po." *Po* is a kind of signal to open your mind and consider a seemingly crazy idea with the hope that doing so will help you turn off your conceptual autopilots. In de Bono's own words, po is a kind of "laxative" for the mind, and its function is to facilitate "rearrangement of information to create new patterns" (1990, 226-27).

So, I've got a po for you. *Po: there is no potential.* Indeed, show me your potential now. Where is this potential you identify with? There's you, on a chair, on a couch, in a recliner, on your bed, or standing on a subway train, reading this book. But where's this potential you talk about? First define it, then show it to me. Put the book down and show yourself your potential right now. Recognize that potential is both a memory of what once was and an imagination of what might be.

Potential is a thought you carry in your mind about yourself. While the word "potential" exists, what it refers to doesn't. What exists is your memory of how you once ran a marathon. What exists is your thought that you still can. But this thought is just a thought that you have right now. A thought about potential isn't potential itself. You are what you are, and there is no other potential you right now next to you. Nor is there is another potential you inside the actual you that you are. Your potential is a vision of possible future accomplishments. Whatever your thoughts of potential are, I hope they materialize. But recognize: however you slice it, your potential is just thoughts of potential. Thoughts are powerful. They lead to action. But you are not your thoughts. Realize that you are not your thoughts of the future. You are not these images in your head, however grounded they are. Recognize that you are not what you think you are yet to become. Conclude: *I am not my (thoughts of) potential. I am not my potential. I am not my image of a future me.*

out of the shadows of time

Neti it out: *I am not my habits. I am not my conditioning.*

When we look at our current selves, we see our past: our habits, our programming, our conditioning, our acquired reflexes, our behavioral defaults, and our autopilots. Ponder all these informational routines, all this baggage of conditioning. Ask yourself: Am I these habits? Am I this echo of my past? To find out, pick one of your habits that you feel would be easy to modify and modify it for a week. Notice that you are still you. Recognize that you are not this habit, that you are not this routine of your past. If you're still not sure, choose a habit that feels a bit more ingrained. Put it on hold for at least a day. Recognize that you are still here, alive and well. Conclude: *I am not my habits. I am not my conditioning. I am not my past.*

choice is a poor choice for identification

Neti it out: *I am not my choices.*

There are two ways in which you are not your choices. Choose the one you like. First, our choices are evidence of what we were, not of what we are; of what we preferred, not of what we prefer; of what we liked, not of what we like. A choice is an act of selection between two or more available options. A choice is an act of the past, however recent that past is. Your choice tells you not about the current you, but about you in the past. Your dating choice, your choice of furniture in your living room, the tattoo you chose, whom you chose to vote for—all these represent a history of varying relevance. You are not your history.

Second, your choice provides information about you—about your values, about your likes and dislikes, about your preferences, goals, and priorities, about your taste and style. You are not any of this information—you are that which this information is about. Try this: with your erasable marker, draw three circles on the mirror, one right after another. If you don't feel like doing it on the mirror, put this book aside and draw three circles, one after another, on three separate pieces of paper. I encourage you not to read on until you've done this, or the exercise will not have an effect.

Now take a look. Did you start each of the circles in the same place? Probably. Did you draw them in the same direction? Probably. Were all three circles roughly of the same diameter/size? Probably. There is a pattern here, right? You seem to have made the same choices three times.

So, here's an important question to ponder: what does this pattern say about you? Maybe something. Maybe nothing. That's the way it is with most choices. Half of them are like dreams we have: meaningless information. The other half seem to have a logic to them, a pattern, some kind of message. Now, ask yourself: am I the circle that I chose? Expand the question: am I the circle of interests that I have chosen? Am I the circle of friends that I've chosen? Of course not. All these circles are just behavioral doodling that expresses your preferences. And your preferences simply express your conditioning, habits, autopilots, programming, previous choices, and all other echoes of your past. Recognize that you are not what you choose, you are the one who is choosing. Choose to dis-identify from your choices. You aren't what your choices say about you. What your choices say about you is just information about you and about your past. You are not information. Conclude: *I am not my choices. My choices are evidence of my past preferences; I am neither my past preferences nor the information they convey about me.* After all, if you are your choices, then who is choosing them?

Breaking Away from the Material Mirror: I Am Not What I Have

Nomadic hunter-gatherers couldn't afford to lug a lot of luggage. They traveled light. Then agriculture developed and changed relationships to things. By settling down, we began to identify with the land that we cultivated and the tools that we cultivated this land with. Surplus of harvests enabled us to possess things that had no pragmatic value. We became hoarders and collectors. We started to identify with what we have. We became possessed by our own possessions. Our own essence began to disappear behind the things that we owned.

self-possession

Neti it out: *I am not what I have or own.*

A true possession is something that cannot be taken away. Everything else is on loan, on lease, in your keeping, under your watch, borrowed and held but not really yours. Everything you claim to be yours can be taken away from you—by a robber, by the IRS, by the stock market, by lawyers, by an "act of God," by revolution, by a regime change. Even your gold teeth aren't safe. Your kidneys can be harvested without your consent. Your mind can be changed without your permission and your ideas can be stolen. Even your identity can be stolen.

So, what is really yours? What is that one aspect of your existence that cannot be taken away from you as long as you are alive? Your essence. Your core self. You own it. It doesn't exist without you. You don't exist without it. You are self-possessed. Recognize: you are not what you have—you are the one who has it. Conclude: *I am not what I own. I am not what I have. I am not what I possess.*

Me/not-me check. Locality question: where are your possessions (your house, your money, your land)? Outside of you. You are not what's outside of you. Permanence question: have you ever lost any money or anything else material? I'll bet you have. Did you vanish? Did you cease to exist? Of course not. Conclude: *I am not the external at my disposal.*

the cost of living

Neti it out: *I am not my assets.*
I am not a reflection of what I have.

Is there anything in your possession that you are willing to die for? Your wallet? Your car? Your house? What thing in your possession are you willing to defend with your life? Your jewelry? Your land? I realize that in the panic of self-defense you might go to mortal combat for whatever it is that is being taken away from you. That's mostly biology and chemistry. That's the jungle in you. I'm not talking about your limbic reflexes. Nor am I talking about protecting your children's assets. When you protect your children's assets or the assets of your significant other, it's not the actual material possessions that you are protecting but their value in assuring the well-being of those you love.

I'm talking about something entirely different. I am asking you to identify a single material asset of yours that exceeds the value of your life. What is more important than your life? A Porsche? A Picasso? Your Mac? The Taj Mahal? *Nothing.* Greater fortunes have been given over at gunpoint for merely an extra breath. This privilege of breath you take for granted is priceless. On some level you know it. Now make it official. Recognize that *you* are your most valued asset. And if this is true, why identify with lesser-value assets? I am not saying that you should up and surrender what you have. Keep what you've rightfully earned, of course. But I am inviting you to recognize the absurdity of equating life with things.

In response to these ideas, you might say that you will not, under any circumstances, give up this or that, *out of principle*. Fine. Let's say that you think along the following lines: "I am this land. My grandparents homesteaded it. I'd give it up only over my dead body." Let's take a look at what this means. You feel this land has a special meaning for you. However, the fact is that this land has no intrinsic meaning. The meaning doesn't come with land. The meaning comes with mind. This land was here long before your grandparents homesteaded it, and it will be here long after your descendants are gone. Land has no landlord. You can put a fence around it. You can pave it over. It still won't be yours. It just is. So, how come it's imbued with such meaning? Where does this meaning come from? From you. From your mind. Your ancestors assigned meaning to this land. You downloaded this software of associations from them as part of your cultural (informational) inheritance, and now you consider the land an integral part of you. It's not.

To help get your mind around this idea, you can do a locality check. Here you stand, on the land, maybe outside of it, perhaps on top of it. Jump up and down to check that the only ties between you and this land are informational, associative, sentimental. That's what you are willing to die for—not for the land, but for the meaning that it has for you. You are willing to die for information. So be it. Your life, your choice. But here's the implication of such a choice. If you are willing to die for an idea, for a principle, for an item of your mind, then you are willing to die for the contents of your consciousness. If so, congratulations. In that case, you do value your internal life more than any of these material possessions. That's quite enlightened of you. But if so, then why identify with lesser, material values on a day-to-day basis? Conclude: *I am not my material assets.* To anchor this idea, try this: take a walk around your material kingdom. Look at everything you have that you feel particularly attached to, everything you identify with. As you proceed, allow yourself the following thought: "If I have to, I am prepared to lose this. I am not this object."

Me/not-me check. I'll leave this up to you. (You've been clearing away the weeds of false identity, wielding a blade of neti-neti in one hand and the me/not-me check in the other like a ninja on meth. I trust that by now you've gotten the hang of it somewhat. So, in the interests of space and to give you some self-directed practice, I'll phase out the me/not-me checks for the time being. I'll remind you to use it now and then, but from this point on, you're on your own. If you're not sure how to apply the locality/permanence questions to weed out false identities from essence, please review the earlier me/not-me checks.)

---

money is silent

Neti it out: *I am not what I make.*

Some people say "Money talks." No, it doesn't. Open your wallet and pull out a twenty. Listen. Money is silent. Money says nothing, not even anything about you.

You are not the money you've saved. You are not the money you've earned. You are not the money you won. You are not money. Money is metal and paper. It clanks, it rustles, but it doesn't talk. If that is so, how can money say anything about you? It doesn't. Your money—however much or little you have of it—is no reflection of you. Money is a crude index of value. We've all come across people with money whom we don't value and people without money whom we do. You are not a reflection of your bank account or lack thereof. Take another long look at that twenty in your wallet. It's a piece of paper that we have all agreed to not tear up. Think about all the hands that have held the piece of paper. Hundreds, thousands of lives came in contact with this piece of paper, and yet it hasn't a darn thing to say about any of the hands that held it. Your cereal box with its nutrition tips has more useful information than this piece of paper. Once again, money doesn't talk. Minds do. So notice this cultural habit of seeking reflection in your earnings, and put this thought out of circulation. Recognize that you aren't a reflection of your income. Income—just like thoughts—comes and goes. But you remain. Conclude: *I am not a reflection of what I make. I am not my income. I am not my earnings. I am not my finances.*

self, not serf

Neti it out: *I am not what I owe. I am not my debt.*

When you lose everything, it might seem that loss is all that's left to identify with. Loss is a situation, not a state of mind. Just like you weren't what you had, you aren't what you lost. Nor are you what you owe. Indenture isn't identity. A financial obligation does not oblige you to identify with your debt. Consider this: Say you owe me money. You agree to pay me back, and you do eventually pay me back. What does that mean? That you have integrity, that you have ethics, that you are true to your word. In other words, you are true to your self.

Debt is an opportunity to manifest yourself in all your self-congruent essence. Paid debt is evidence of a self that knows how not to run from itself. So, if you are buried in debt, and you are meeting your financial obligations, even if the world still owns everything but your essence, consider yourself in the process of getting a great bargain. After all, payment after payment, you are paying for the privilege to be true to yourself. And, if you are paying down your debt (no matter how slowly), apparently that action merits the costs. After all, anything of value has a cost. If you are meeting your financial obligations, you are paying for your peace of mind and for a sense of integrity, which are obviously worth every penny you owe. Recognize that the fact of the debt has much less to say about you than what you are doing about it. Recognize that even if you sometimes feel like a serf, you are still a self. Conclude: *I am not my debt.*

a full empty bowl

Neti it out: *I am not my financial independence.*

Many spiritual traditions speak of humility. Some build it into a meditation practice. In your travels you might have seen a monk's begging bowl. Sitting before this often-empty bowl is an opportunity for the monk to divest himself of the distraction of pride. So, while his bowl may be physically empty, it is actually full of humility and the simplicity that state brings.

Being financially "self-made" remains a hallmark of modern-day achievement. And, yet, financial independence is a poor substitute for psychological (identity-based) independence. Let's get clear: you are not the money that you have, no matter how much of it you have and how autonomously and honestly you came by it. To dis-identify from your financial independence, from your pride in financial self-sufficiency, I invite you to set a precedent of experiencing yourself as psychologically self-made, even if you are financially dependent. I know this exercise may be asking a lot from you. You will need to take a risk, which can be uncomfortable for some people. But I believe that taking that risk will bring you many benefits of dis-identification.

Whenever you are ready, whenever you're in a place with pedestrian traffic, consider asking a passerby for money. You don't need to carry a "Will work for money" sign. I'm talking about one small precedent. For example: ask for a quarter for the parking meter. Recognize that in setting this begging precedent you are dis-identifying from a whole handful of things: a) you are letting go of any pride you have in your financial independence, b) you are letting go of any concern about what a random mind might think of you, and c) you are giving yourself an opportunity to let go of any self-loathing thoughts you might have. That's a good deal on top of the free quarter you might score.

Now, if this sounds way past your comfort threshold, consider a more sublimated version of begging. You've seen those Salvation Army donation collectors ringing bells during the holidays? Become one. Set a precedent of financial humility to turbo-charge your dis-identification from what you have. Conclude: *I am not my pride. I am not my financial independence.*

get nomadic

Neti it out: *I am not my creature comforts.*

Go camping to meditate on your independence of all your creature comforts. Live a day or a weekend or a week in the wilderness. Go alone, if you're a competent camper, or in the company of a guide or more-experienced friend. Learn from your survival experience. Tap into that ancient nomadic part of you that just walks the path without having to own it. Recognize that you are your own home. You are your own abode. Understand that you are not the material walls around your life—you are the one who lives there. Conclude: *I am not my creature comforts. I am not my home.*

information ownership

Neti it out: *I am not my legacy.*

Donating money, resources, or time in exchange for a plaque or a mention isn't charity. Rather, it's self-promotion. So give something away and, along with it, give away your identification with others' approval. Give away a piece of that ego-self and thereby feel enriched in your essence. Recognize that you are not the informational trace you leave in others' minds. You aren't your informational halo—you are the source of that light. So shine on without reflectors. Why own information in random minds when you are trying to get your own information out of your way? Make a donation, but do it anonymously. Dare to remain nameless. Conclude: *I am not my legacy. I am not my reputation.*

Breaking Away from the Relational Mirror: I Am Not My Role

Role identification is pervasive. In the game of dis-identification, the relational mirror is one of the hardest to walk away from. And yet, getting distance from this mirror is especially important. Becoming subsumed by your relational roles is a quick way to lose your sense of self.

Dis-identification from a relational role doesn't mean an abandonment of the role. Not at all. Recall that dis-identification is not detachment. It's differentiation, individuation, a return to self. Relationships—both healthy and unhealthy—can tend to overwhelm us. We go from being ourselves to being primarily husbands, wives, partners, fiancés, and so on. We redefine ourselves as mothers, fathers, daughters, or sons and wind up getting stuck in our roles.

As rewarding as these roles may be, roles—like all identities—reduce our complexity and stereotype our uniqueness. Instead of consulting ourselves, we start to defer to norms with a given role. Roles rely on rules. Rules rely on repetition. Repetition relies on mindlessness. Mindlessness leads to the loss of self.

Jettison the relational disguise. Shed the layer of role-bound obligations. Excavate your true self from underneath the rubble of relational expectations. Dis-identify from formality to reconnect with your essence. A role is a script, a part played rather than a life lived. So, as you begin to dis-identify from your scripted behavior, expect more (not less) emotional intimacy and authenticity of engagement. However, if you meet resistance when you choose to step out of a role, accept it as feedback about what others think about the importance of you being you.

the present is unrelated to the past

Neti it out: *I am not my relational history.*

We often identify with the history of our relationships. However, history is only information. Recall that the past doesn't exist. What exists is our memory of the past. You won't find the past anywhere except for in the informational archives of our minds.

Identification is the equation of one thing to another. But how do you relate something that exists (the present) to something that doesn't (the past)? These two—the present and the past—are unrelated. You are no more your relational history than you are any history. You are not what was; you are what is. You are not an "ex." You are not a divorcée. You are not somebody's high-school sweetheart. You are not the relationships you've been in. You are not the relationships you wanted but couldn't have. You are not whom you left or divorced or cheated on. You are not who left you, divorced you, or cheated on you. You are not whom you loved or who loved you. You are not who abused you or whom you saved. You are not any of your past romantic affiliations. Right now, none of that exists. You will not find any of that right now anywhere in this endless universe. All there is right now is memory of what was and wasn't.

But you are not memory. These memories ebb and flow, but you remain. These thoughts about what was and wasn't come and leave, but you remain. Relate to that. Relate to what's always there. Relate to this sense of presence that you have preserved and carried through all the pages of your relational history. Relationships are relative. Like everything, in this impermanent world, they change. But this sense of presence, this indisputable fact of self-existence, this unmistakable and self-evident fabric of you-being-you, is absolute. It remains the same regardless of its relational context. Conclude: *I am not my relationship history.*

relating vs. co-existing

Neti it out: *I am not a "we." I am not a proxy self.*

Recall that the word "identity" means sameness. Thus, to identify with another person is to draw a sign of equation, a sign of sameness, between two people who are obviously not the same. When we identify with someone, we say and think in terms of similarities. We say "I am just like that," or "We have the same interests," or "We are quite alike." Note that the language of identification is also the language of relationships. When we identify with somebody, we might say or think "I can relate to that." Indeed, to identify and to relate are pretty much the same thing. All relationships are inherently identifications. Therein lies the problem.

Relationships tend to erase interpersonal boundaries. This gradual process of taking down the fences between the two parties is the very process of psychological intimacy. It's no surprise; the word "union" does, after all, stem from the word "one." As you see, a relationship, by virtue of its unifying pull, is an inherent threat to uniqueness. As you orbit one another, you begin to talk alike, think alike, and even look like each other. A shared identity emerges: "I" yields to "we." This isn't a good thing or a bad thing, it's just a thing. The dynamics of intimacy parallel those of gravity. It's just the physics of love.

But let's take a closer look at what can be done to manage over-identification. We'll look at two scenarios starring two people, each with an "I" of their own.

Scenario 1. One person's sense of self subsumes another person's sense of self. In other words, one person completely identifies with the other and ceases to exist as a separate entity. What's left is one "I," which begins to function as a "we." To reiterate, in this scenario a stronger self psychologically cannibalizes the weaker self, leading to the two selves collapsing into one. The result is an undemocratic "we" in which only one "I" has a real voice and the other "I" votes a straight party line.

Scenario 2. Both partners in the relationship retain their separate sense of self, their "I," and manage to develop a shared identity, a democratic "we," in which both have an equal vote.

So, here's my question: what's going on in your primary relationship? Are you still there? Are you still an "I," or have you disappeared inside the psychological collective of a "we"? If so, do you have an equal vote, or are you kept in line by the party whip? Or, as the case may be, are you calling the shots for both of you? Are you the commander in chief, thinking, feeling, wanting, deciding, leading for both of you? Are you the entire "we" or are you still you? Take an evening or two to examine your relational dynamics. Weigh the pros and cons of over-identification with your significant other or the pros and cons of having your significant other over-identify with you. If you find that the two of you have disappeared into some kind of "we," if you conclude that either you or your partner ceased to exist as a separate entity, ask yourself: who am I in a relationship with? With my proxy self?

To drive this point home, consider the following mirror exercise. Position yourself in front of a full-size mirror. Notice your reflection. Now walk up to the mirror. Press yourself against it. Notice your reflection disappear. Ponder this peculiar tension between intimacy and identity.

Consider stepping back—literally and metaphorically. Consider the psychological hyphenation of co-existence. I am not suggesting that you hyphenate your last names. That's the *form* of co-existence, not the essence of it. Co-existence is inter-being. A co-journeying, a co-operation, a bi-partisanship. Weigh the pros and cons of infusing some self-space back into your relationship so that you can discover yourself and your partner anew. If you feel you have been subsumed by the relationship, start saying "I" now and then; dare to express a preference. If you feel that you're the only one making decisions and expressing opinions in this relationship, take a break. Let your partner drive for a bit.

You can also try this: get two hand-held mirrors and hold them in front of each other. Notice the infinite regress. Study it. Notice that as each mirror is reflected in the other, it is diminished and reduces in size at each phase of counter-reflection. Bring the mirrors closer to each other and notice the counter-reflections stifle and diminish. Bring the mirrors even closer until they touch. See this union of surfaces cancel each other. Pull the mirrors apart: notice the reflections expand and breathe deeper.

Recognize that this sameness between the two of you is relative, contrived, habitual. Recall the time when you were interested in your partner's uniqueness and not just in the ways that the two of you were similar. Recognize that a mirror looking at a mirror reflects nothing new. Break away from this infinite, diminishing regress of similarities to re-experience each other anew. Conclude: *I am not a "we." I am not a proxy self. I am not a reflection of a reflection. I am not another's mirror.* Share your insights with your partner.

to dis-identify from other is to re-identify with self

Neti it out: *I am not my relationship.*

To dis-identify from your significant other is not to abandon them but to renew a connection with your abandoned sense of self. Discuss the importance of time alone (self-time) with your partner and claim it. Go shopping by yourself. Watch a movie by yourself. Have a night out with your own friends. You aren't joined at the hip. You don't have to be joined at the mind, either. Discuss your thinking behind this with your partner, offer some context to prevent misunderstanding, and go on a date with yourself. Recognize that you are not your relationships. You are *in* a relationship. You are not a relationship. Relationship is a circumstance, where you're at socially, romantically—not what you are. Conclude: *I am not my relationship.*

starring in your own show

Neti it out: *I am not my role.*

Life, unlike theatre, is the kind of drama that comes without dress-rehearsal, encores, or repeat performances. Everything is once. That's why we can't afford to follow someone else's script.

A role is an expectation, a cultural blueprint of how you should be. A role is a norm, a set of standards, a code of conduct. It has nothing to do with you. It wasn't written with you in mind. A role is a one-size-fits-all behavioral mold.

Catalog your roles. Interview your significant other as to what he or she expects of you. Review the script before your next repeat performance. Ask yourself: is this me? Am I these expectations? Recognize that you are not a relational puppet. Flail your arms—see? No strings. Recognize that you are not the relational groove you are in; you are the wheel, and you can spin this life in any direction you see fit. Recognize that you are not starring in somebody else's show for the benefit of the audience. Take the relational mask off to see your original face. Follow your own lead. Star in your own show. Be your own protagonist or run the risk of leaving a legacy of being an inessential extra. Conclude: *I am not my role.*

dynamics are dynamic

Neti it out: *I am not my relational status.*

Life is fluid. Nothing is static—not even your relational status. Relationships are dynamics and therefore are ever-evolving. You might think you are a fiancé, a husband, a wife, a friend, or a partner. Are you? Is this relational status guaranteed? A promise of living together forever is a statement of intent, not a guarantee. A wedding band binds the capillary blood circulation in your partner's finger but not his or her free will. So, before you get into a habit of introducing yourself as, say, Bob's wife, Suzie, perhaps you can keep the original sequence: you aren't Bob's wife, Suzie; you are Suzie, Bob's wife. Place the emphasis on you, not on your relational status. Conclude: *I am not my relational status.*

---

child-parent

Neti it out: *I am not my generational or functional status.*

Being a parent is an identity with a seemingly lifelong half-life. What is a parent? I guess there are two ways to look at this: biologically and functionally. You are biologically a parent if you have contributed your genetic material to the emergence of another human being. This, of course, is a purely formal way of looking at the matter. Scores of fathers beget children without knowing that they did. Men and women donate and sell their genes in the form of sperm and eggs that are then combined in a manner anatomically unrelated to them. Surrogate mothers birth other people's children. And legions upon legions of biological parents knowingly abandon their children, sell them to others, or abuse them in a variety of ways that do not fit the functional definition of a parent.

The functional idea of parenting would be, at its most basic level, caregiving. And this functional frame seems like the most appropriate way to look at parenting non-formally. A parent is a person who extends care. However, this functional definition muddies up the waters even more. Innumerable adults who provide logistical care to their children end up being psychologically parented by their own offspring. And not during a late-life role reversal, but during the prime child-rearing years. You have probably encountered these "little adults" sounding wise beyond their years because they have been hard at work serving to validate and mirror to their own reflection-seeking parents. This kind of "parentification," for example, is common among the children of narcissists. These kids' sole purpose, it seems, is to reflect their parents in a favorable light.

So, what we have here is a rather ambiguous concept. What does it really mean to be a parent? Are you a parent because you have a generational advantage over your offspring? Are you a parent because you provide your children with logistical care? Are you a parent if you are a biologically and logistically unrelated adult (say, a therapist, family friend, school counselor, or neighbor) who has made some pivotal emotional contributions to a given child's life? I hope that you are beginning to see the fuzziness of this identification. Technically, like anything else, being a parent is a role. Regardless of how well or poorly you play it, a role is still a role—that is, something that you do a set of expectations and behaviors that you fulfill. You are not what you do: you are not your performance, your actions, your duties, or your achievements. You are the one who *does* all of that. So, from the functional standpoint, you are not a parent even if you are a great one. You are not a function.

Now, if you insist that you are a parent because you've given birth to a child or contributed sperm to create a child, then what we're dealing with is a kind of identification in which you base your identity on a particular moment of the past. Yes, at some point your physiology was involved in a manner that produced an offspring. As special a moment as that might have been, the fact is that we are talking about something in the past. Recall that there is no past. There's our memory of it: baby pictures, a shaky video from the delivery room, tangible and intangible information about that event. But you aren't giving birth right now. You aren't impregnating anyone right now. (I certainly hope not, or I'd have to ask about what you are doing reading this book if you are so engaged otherwise.) So, this kind of generational identification with oneself as a parent because at some point in the past you have produced an offspring is a case of being stuck in the mirror of time.

Recognize that you are not a parent. Being a parent is what you do, but you are not what you do. This dis-identification doesn't have to diminish your connection to whomever you care for. On the contrary. As you will discover, it's by being more yourself that you stand to offer more to others. Any role, whether it's that of a friend or a parent, inevitably limits and restricts the scope of our essence. Dis-identifying from your role as a parent allows you to re-identify with the aspects of yourself you have abandoned. By re-integrating those split-off parts of yourself, you stand to be a more meaningful presence in your child's life. Conclude: *I am not my generational status. I am not my parenting role. I am not a role. I am not a parent—that's what I do, but I am not what I do.* Nor are you a child for that matter. The same arguments apply. Think it through on your own. Conclude: *I am not a child.* Bottom line: you are not your generational or functional status.

Breaking Away from the Mirror of Bio-Data: I Am Not My Body

So, stripped of all kinds of false identities, you stand naked in front of yet another, very convincing mirror—the mirror of your body. "Surely," you might be thinking right now, "he's not going to try to convince me that I am not my body." Oh yes, I will. Are you ready for another round of identity-detox rumble? I think you are. So, put 'em up and let's duke it out.

Worry not: there is no identity to bruise here. There is no body between us. I assure you: you'll come out of this neti-neti mud wrestle cleaner than before. Not dis-embodied, of course, but at least slightly dis-identified from this fleshy bastion in which you've been barricaded. And before the lotus of your identity emerges out of these murky waters of somatic identification, a tip from Anthony de Mello: "Don't burn your body, burn the ego" (1984, 102). Indeed, you need your body. You just don't need to keep confusing your essential self with it.

what body?

Neti it out: *I am not what I identify with. I am not my body.*

Milan Kundera, in *The Unbearable Lightness of Being*, offers this insight: "A long time ago, man would listen in amazement to the sound of regular beats in his chest, never suspecting what they were. He was unable to identify himself with so alien and unfamiliar an object as the body. The body was a cage, and inside that cage was something which looked, listened, feared, thought, and marveled; that something, that remainder left over after the body had been accounted for, was the soul" (1999, 40). Indeed, we know our body as information that we live inside of. Close your eyes, and ask yourself: what is the evidence that I have a body? Notice that all you are able to come up with is information. With your eyes closed, keep asking yourself: "How do I know that I have a body?" Recognize that all you come up with is thoughts, feelings, and sensations such as "I feel my hand move" and "I know I am inside my body right now" and "If I didn't have a body, why would I have an itch right now?"

You aren't thoughts about your body, you aren't feelings about your body, you aren't the sensations you have. You are that which is aware of all this internal information. With your eyes open, look at your body. Touch it. Recognize that you are not what you see or feel or touch. All this is just sensory information. You are not this information, you are the one processing it. Clip a fingernail. Look at the clipping. Is that you? Pick a hair out of your brush. Look at it. Is that you? Realize that no single part of you is you. Realize that identification with the body isn't a given but something we learn. Infants, for example, scare themselves with their own limbs before they learn to identify these external appendages as parts of themselves. Recognize that body identification is just an ingrained informational habit. Conclude: *I am not that which I identify with. I am not my body.*

your body is a distraction from your self

Neti it out: *I am not my body image.*

Your body feeds you sensory data. In so doing, it distracts you from yourself. Here's how Willard Johnson, the author of *Riding the Ox Home*, conveys this idea: "Our sense of identity gradually builds around the experiences we accumulate on the constantly recording memory... In the meditatively unpracticed individual, this process of the sensory-motor domination of consciousness is never interrupted, but continues until death. Such consciousness rarely stands outside itself in ecstasy, never glimpsing its spiritual dimension... Its deepest level of mind remains 'unrealized'" (1982, 83). Indeed, the body is a memory and sensory input.

Try this: close your eyes and ask yourself, *how do I know my body?* Notice that various images of your body appear. Recognize that you know your body by way of memory, that you carry with you a mental representation of what you look like. Recognize that you are not these thoughts and images of how you look; you are not this mental representation of yourself. You are not information. Conclude: *I am not my body image. I am not this picture of my body that I see in my mind.*

George Washington's axe

Neti it out: *I am not my body.*

Here is a version of a paradox that has seen many incarnations. Let's say that an antique collector happens to be in possession of "George Washington's axe." In the years since it was actually owned by George Washington, however, it has had its handle replaced three times and was twice fitted with a new head. Thus, no original part remains. Is it still "George Washington's axe"?

As you ponder this, recall that you too have been replaced and refitted on a cellular level a time or two, at the very least. So tell me: whose body is this? Who owns it? Who is in charge of this bio-mass? Nobody? Is it just a body on its own? Just a body self-possessed? If so, then why do you call it yours? If so, then why do you identify with it? And, if you identify with your body, you're saying that you are your body. If you are your body then who is there to claim it as yours? To claim this body as yours, you'd have to be separate from it. If you are separate from it, then you are not your body. So, whose body is it? Yours or not yours? If not yours, then who's reading this book, who's holding this book, who's pondering this, and, most importantly, what for? My guess is that you claim this body as yours. If so, then you have no option but to conclude: *I am not my body.*

---

one-way river

Neti it out: *I am not this body.*

Heraclitus, one of the great Greek philosophers, proclaimed: you cannot enter the same river twice. Indeed, a river, like time, flows but in one direction. Even if you step into it at the exact same spot on shore, the water will be different.

Your body is like a river in its never-ceasing flow of cellular change. If the river of your body never stands still, then where is this stand-alone body form to identify with? Where's this body of yours when, by the time you call it "this," it is already different? Whichever body you have, it is never this body. Whichever body you claim as yours, it's the memory of a body you are claiming. Sure, you don't see the change, but you know it's there. So, why fool yourself by identifying with the body you don't have? Why be stuck in the mirror of body-time?

Try to beat the clock. Try to say "this body" fast enough to beat your cellular division to the punch. Realize that in the time it takes for you to say "this body" you will have undergone an astronomical number of changes on a cellular level and an incalculable number of changes on the level of micro (sub-atomic) particles. Recognize that what you are identifying with is information about how your body was a second ago. As brief as this lapse of time is, a memory is a memory. As I see it, you have no option but to conclude: *I am not this body memory.*

a whole

Neti it out: *I am not a sum of my body parts.*

You've heard the phrase: the whole is greater than the sum of its parts. Your body is parts, and you are the whole. If you are greater than your body, you are not your body parts. You are not your face, your hair, your hips, your breasts, your legs, your butt, your nose, your eyes, your lips, your stomach, your feet, your neck, your waist, your teeth, your brows, your hands, your calves, your back, or your skin. So, whatever body part you like or dislike, whatever aspect of your physique you represent yourself with or feel ashamed of, you are not that part. Conclude: *I am not my body parts.*

why identify with that which you cannot fully control?

Neti it out: *I am not my body.*

A poet of ancient India, Devara Dasimayya, asks: "If this is my body, would it not follow my will?" (Ramanujan 1973, 98). Keeping this in mind, consciously try to grow a hair. Or, grow a nail. How about an extra finger? If this is your body, then how come you are not in complete control of it? An intriguing proposition, isn't it?

But let's be careful and not take it too far. Of course your body is yours—but only up to a point. As we all know, our bodies seem to have an agenda of their own, doing whatever they are doing without consulting us. So, why is it that we so fully identify with our bodies when we obviously can't completely control them? Why identify with an ocean? We can sail it, we can break some of its waves, but we cannot entirely control it. Wouldn't that which we call "self" have to be, by definition, responsive to its own self-government? To keep identifying so fully with something we cannot fully control smacks of those codependent relationships in which one partner keeps trying to change the other. A dysfunctional arrangement. Recognize that you are not that which you cannot fully control. Conclude: *I am not my body.*

happy breath-day

Neti it out: *I am not my age.*

How old are you? Not to the year, but to the day, to the minute, to the second, to the time zone? Age tells you nothing about the essential you. Sure, age says something about your body, but you are not your body. Your age is a time stamp on the envelope of your body. You aren't the envelope; you are the letter inside.

Set a precedent: skip your birthday. If you want to have a party, have a party. Instead of celebrating your age, celebrate the present moment. Set a precedent of dating yourself as older than you are. Recognize that nothing changes about you when you do that. See through the cheap flattery of being carded. Somebody's taking you to be younger than you chronologically are says more about that person's observation skills than it says about you. When somebody assesses you as chronologically younger than you are, they give you nothing but a piece of their ill-informed mind. It's the same when someone thinks you're older than you are. Matter-of-factly correct their misperception.

Explain that *actually you are ageless,* and proceed with the only time designation that matters—this moment. Recognize that you are not this age or that age. You are now. If you are mindfully present, then you are fully and timelessly alive. That's your age; moment-old, reborn with every breath. Happy breath-day. Conclude: *I am not my age. My age is a crude index of vitality: I am not this time stamp.*

---

transcend your origins

Neti it out: *I am not my origins.*

Race is a major platform for self-identification. But face it: genetically, we are all mutts. (If you don't know what I mean, try watching *National Geographic: The Human Family Tree* with Spencer Wells, a show from 2009 that retraces our genes to one and the same point of origin in East Africa.)

Are you your pigment, the amount of melanin in your skin? Are you willing to identify yourself exclusively and exhaustively with the landscape of your facial features? What is the real-time relevance of all of this to you as you're reading this very sentence? Are you willing to exchange your individuality for circumstances, context, and history? Ask yourself: *who am I outside these contextual definitions?* What race, ethnicity, or culture are you in that gap in between your thoughts or when you stand bewildered, in awe of all that is interrelated? Origins are your past. You are not your past. You are now. *Dare* to conclude: *I am not my ethnicity, my race, my clan, my tribe, my origins.*

---

beyond gender

Neti it out: *I am not my gender.*

Gender is a curious thing. First, gender can be changed. If an aspect of your self can be changed, it fails to meet our criterion of permanence. If your gender can be changed, you are not your gender. Second, we are all anatomically the same until about eight weeks of gestation, at which point some of us biologically differentiate into males and some of us continue on the path toward development as females (Bertrand, Rappaport, and Sizonenko 1993). If, as a guy, you are new to this information, just ask yourself what those two nipples are doing on your chest. Ponder this. Third, societies of all degrees of sophistication continue to promote gender roles. Ask yourself how strong your identification with gender would be if you had grown up on a deserted island without anyone modeling to you how to be a girl or a boy. Fourth: some people think they are one gender but are living in a body of the opposite sex. Imagine that for a second. Say you are biologically a female but you feel you are a male. Now, flip that around: you are biologically a male but you feel you are a female. Just because most of us have been spared this tumultuous predicament, it doesn't mean that we should ignore the writing on the wall. The very possibility of thinking that your gender doesn't match your body suggests that gender identity is unrelated to sex. What this means is that there are two dis-identification angles here. We have already established that you are not your body. Neither are you any of the characteristics of your body, be it height, weight, age, or biological gender. And now, as evidenced by the fact that gender identity is unrelated to anything truly essential to you, you can also dis-identify from gender identity. It's just another informational identity layer.

Do you *need* to dis-identify from your gender? Not necessarily. If you feel trapped by gender roles, then dis-identify away. Recognize that you are inside this body like a hand in a glove. Whether the glove is made of velvet or leather is a description of the glove, not of the hand that's in it. The poet Dasimayya reminds us: "Look, the self that hovers in between is neither man nor woman" (Ramanujan 1973, 27). Conclude: *gender is information about my role in this culture. Sex is information about body. I am not information about my body. I am not my gender.*

surviving the medical classifications

Neti it out: *I am not my disease, diagnosis,*
prognosis, or medical history.

Health used to be a qualitative description. You felt good or you felt bad. That was about it. It's different nowadays: we know our health status and over-identify with it. There's a danger in that. Not to our body, but to our sense of self.

(I know I'm going to step on a few toes here, but I'm going to do it anyway. That's the kind of book this is.) We've come to identify ourselves with the diseases that we've survived. If you survived, say, cancer, that's wonderful. I'm truly glad for you. But let me ask you this: is it really useful to you to refer to yourself as "cancer survivor"? Perhaps, on some level, if the illness were to re-occur (God forbid), the knowledge that you survived it before would help you mount your defenses. But it's not as though you're really at risk of forgetting. You can still remember your past struggle and use the memory of your survival to leverage your immune defenses next time—all without having to identify with your survivor status. Why reduce your marvelous complexity to a record of the battles you won? There's more to you than your health status. Why be a medical statistic? Ponder this for whatever it is worth. If you find a way in which identifying with your health status helps you, then by all means, keep this identification. But if you don't, then ditch this medical ID. The same argument goes for any ongoing medical issue that you have. For example, why call yourself "stage such-and-such of such-and-such cancer"? You are not a stage of cancer or a type of diabetes or your HIV status. Your herpes, your arthritis, your amputation status, your disability status— all this is simply information about your health. You are not your health information. Conclude: *I am not my health status. I am not my medical history. I am not my diagnosis. I am not my prognosis. I am not a disease. I am not my disease status.*

orient inside

Neti it out: *I am not my sexual orientation.*

Find a light switch. Flip it with your right hand. Flip it with your left hand. Put a leather glove on. Flip the light switch. Take the leather glove off and put a rubber glove on instead. Flip the switch.

Where am I going with this? Here: you are not what you turn on, nor are you what turns you on. You aren't straight. You aren't gay. You aren't bisexual. All this is information about what you like to do with your body and whom you're likely to fall in love with. You aren't what you do with your body, and you aren't your romances. You are you. Consciousness is asexual. Indeed, sexual orientation is nothing but a vector of your libido. You aren't where you look or what you look at—you are that which is looking. Identification with sexual orientation is dis-orientation, a confusion of form with essence. You aren't whom you love, you are the one who loves. So, no need to base your sense of self on the gender of the hand that turns you on. Identify with the light itself that shines when you are turned on. Conclude: *I am not my sexual orientation.*

zhuangzi

Neti it out: *I am not this body/mind.*

Zhuangzi, a Daoist sage, once had a dream of being a butterfly. Upon awakening, he pondered: "Am I Zhuangzi dreaming that I am a butterfly, or am I a butterfly dreaming that I am Zhuangzi?" (Tzu 2007). Are you a body dreaming that you are a mind, or are you a mind dreaming that you are a body? A mind? A body? Both? Neither? Recognize that whatever you'll think in response to this question will be just that—a thought. Whatever the answer, you are not your answer. Whatever you choose to identify with, you are not your identification. However you decide to describe yourself (body, mind, body-mind, mindbody), you are not the description but that which you are describing. Conclude: *I am not this. I am not that.*

---

mario

Neti it out: *I am not my body.*

I was twenty-one when I played my first video game. Having grown up in the Soviet Union, I had zero exposure to this type of entertainment. So, here I was, getting a crash course in how to use a game controller from my girlfriend. The game was Super Mario. When the game started and I found Mario precariously perched on a floating platform, I vanished. I became Mario. I/Mario stepped back to time my leap forward to another floating platform and went for it. I/Mario didn't make it. As I/Mario fell into the abyss, my *body* gasped. In a moment, I realized the significance of what had just happened. I (now just I, no longer Mario) instantly appreciated the dis-embodying power of immersion. My body's reaction reflected what happened on the screen, to Mario. As far as my body was concerned, I, not Mario, had fallen off the floating platform. Comical, but no big deal: this kind of effect is commonplace.

Here's what's of interest. The reason my body experienced the fall is because, when I took the controller into my hands, I unwittingly dis-identified from my body and identified with the body of my onscreen avatar (Mario). If I hadn't temporarily dis-identified from my body, my body would not have experienced the fall the way it did. Lesson learned: dis-identification from the body is possible and common. We do it all the time. Without this kind of dis-identification, there would be no immersion-style video games or blockbuster thrillers. We dis-identify from our body every time we push ourselves to get on a treadmill. So, close your eyes and run this thought through your mind: *I am not this body.* Why seek identity in that which you can dis-identify from?

you are not a number

Neti it out: *I am not my weight.*

What is your weight? I mean not the weight of your body but of your essence, of whatever it is that you consider to be you. Not the weight of your muscles, your bones, your connective tissues, your fluids, the fillings in your teeth, and all the food in your digestive tract. I'm talking about the weight of *you*, of that which is reading this right now. How much does that weigh? Nothing? Your essence is weightless? If so, then there is no number on your bathroom scale to register your weight.

Recognize that you—not your body, but your essential self—aren't quantifiable. Close your eyes. Ask: "How much does the one asking this very question weigh?" Recognize it's not your bones asking, or your muscles, or your connective tissues, or your fluids, or your dental fillings, or the food in your stomach. All of that is silent. Your body has no way of "weighing in on" this question because it has nothing to do with you. Of course, you don't have to forego your wellness goals. Just forego your identification with all this meaningless calorie-counting and weighing nonsense. Conclude: *I am not my weight.*

metamorphosis

Neti it out: *I am not my form.*

In Franz Kafka's story "The Metamorphosis," first published in 1915, the protagonist's body turns into a cockroach. But that's not the point. The point is that nothing else changes. The protagonist (and his neuroticism) remains the same. This is the irony of change. Change happens against the backdrop of the changeless. As the body ages, to a large extent we still feel the same inside. As the body ages, the gap between our physical age and how old we feel inside seems to continually widen. Why not listen to this sense of internal sameness? Metamorphosis is a change of form, not of essence. You aren't what's changing, you are that which remains the same. Conclude: *I am not my physical form.*

Breaking Away from the Mirror of Language: I Am Not a Word

Two prehistoric apes stand in the tall grass. One points a finger in a certain direction to alert the other to a crouching tiger that is about to prey on them, as if to say: "Watch out. Tiger." Language developed from the behavior of finger-pointing. Each word is an attempt to point to and to point out. The finger was the first "this" (if pointing something *out*) and the first "there" (if pointing *to* something). The finger was the first tongue. But, as Buddhists say, the finger pointing to the moon isn't the moon. The entire mind is a drop-down menu of verbal gestures that self-select—associatively, compulsively, reflexively, reactively, mechanically, robotically, and mostly unconsciously—in an attempt to name the nameless.

But no matter how many fingers we point at reality, no matter how many words we use to describe it, a finger pointing at the moon still isn't the moon, and a word isn't its referent. No "this" ever equals the *that* it points to. You are part of this inexpressible reality. So, why fear words if they cannot describe us? Recognize that when seeking a reflection of what you are in language, all you find is language, not you. You aren't any given description, you are that which you are trying to describe—that which remains when all descriptions have failed. You are not a word.

nameless

Neti out your name.

You're born nameless. Your name isn't a given—it is given. So let's neti it out. Write your name down. Look at it. Recognize that you are not this collection of symbols. Say your name out loud. Recognize that you are not this sound. Think your name. Recognize that you are not this thought. Recognize that your name is nothing but a word. Embrace your essential namelessness. Conclude: *I am not my name.*

Me/not-me check. Permanence question: would you cease to exist if you changed your name? Of course not. Conclude: *I am not how I am known.*

I-less-ness

Neti "I" out.

Close your eyes and keep asking yourself "What is 'I'?" Note the quotation marks. The question isn't "What am I?" but "What is 'I'?" Recognize that "I" is a word and that you are not a word. Recognize that any English-speaking person uses the word "I" to refer to himself. So how can this word exclusively apply to you? How can this commonly used pronoun have anything essential to say about you? Recognize that you are not this word, not this sound, not this symbol. Understand that you are the I-less-ness behind the word "I." Conclude: *I am not the word "I."*

not "me," not "me"

Neti "me" out.

The word "me" is the oblique form of the pronoun "I." The oblique case is a view from the side. "Me" is what you'd see if you were looking at yourself from the side. Ask yourself: who is this who is looking at herself from the side and sees "me?" You know when you do something that seems characteristic of you, you might say, "That's me. That's just like me." No, that's not. You are not *how* you are, you are not what typifies you, you are not what describes you, you are not the words you use to refer to yourself. Recognize that you are not a "me." "Me" is a just a word. Conclude: *I am not the word "me."*

lift the veil of words

Neti it out: *I am not the words of my self-descriptions.*

Coat a stick with red paint and look at it. What are you seeing— a red stick? Not really: the actual stick has disappeared under a coat of red paint. You are looking at a particular distribution of red paint in space, not at the stick. Sure, you know that the stick is still there. But the stick itself is no longer visible. So, when you think you're seeing a stick, you are actually looking at your own thought of the stick.

Words are just like paints. Once we label a given something, we stop seeing that something and begin seeing our description of it. Meditate on how this relates to you. Consider what parts of you may have disappeared under the paint of your self-descriptions. Conclude: *I am not this verbal paint that I cover myself with. I am not the words of my self-descriptions.*

nothing to point at

Neti it out: *I am not any verbal or non-verbal representation.*

Ask yourself: *what am I?* Try to answer this without saying or writing anything down. What are your options? Well, you could draw yourself. Go ahead. Look at the drawing. Are you this drawing? No. Try taking a picture of yourself. Go on. Look at the picture. Are you this picture? No. You could record your breathing. Try it. Now listen to the sounds. Are you these sounds? Nope. What else could you do? What if you point a finger at yourself? Go ahead. Look at what the finger is pointing at. Perhaps it's pointing at the skin of your chest, or the skin of your face, or the skin of your head. Are you this skin? No. This skin is part of you (until it sloughs off and regenerates), but you are not this skin. Perhaps you'll pull out an X-ray or a brain scan (probably not, but hey, maybe you have these things in your basement). Are you the resulting X-ray picture or scan? No. Where are you? Show me this invisible you. Show you to you. Recognize: you are not anything you can verbally or nonverbally point at. Conclude: *I am not any verbal or nonverbal representation of me.*

close the book on language

Neti out any verbal self-reference.

Ponder the following: the only way to answer the question "What/who am I?" is through words. Get a dictionary and browse through it. As you see various words that apply to you, realize that you are not these words. Make it real: put a finger on the word on the page. Realize: you are here; the word is there. Then think the word. Recognize that you are not the word you are thinking because you are not a thought. Conclude: *I am not any word.*

the language of silence

Neti it out: *I am not my language.*

What language are you? Notice how we link our origin to our language. The English speak English. Italians speak Italian. Russians speak Russian. Historically, we identify with our language. Makes sense: we think in it. But do we?

Ask yourself this: what language is image? What language is memory? What language is fear? And, most importantly, what language is silence? As you're reading this sentence, like a tireless hound with its nose to the ground of this page, your mind is following the scent of what I'm communicating with these words, sniffing out meaning as it goes. But what happens to all this mind's chatter when you flip the pages, when you're in between reading and information processing?

Notice the silence of your mind. What language is that? What about all those moments of pure awareness, like when you simply lie on your bed, staring at the ceiling, not really thinking anything? In what language does your mind go blank? Recognize that if you can exist outside of language (perhaps as you've done as you've paused to ponder this thought), then it's time to sever this umbilical cord of linguistic identification. Conclude: *I am not my language.*

a linguistic bodymind workout

Neti it out: *I am not my language.*

Here's a sweatless linguistic workout for your bodymind. As you finish reading this exercise, try tapping your hands intermittently (left, right, left, right) ten times, counting odd numbers in one language and even numbers in another language. Try it a few times.

Now, let me ask you this: in which language were you choosing to switch from one language to another? That's right: recall how you would say "one" in one language and "two" in the other language. Each time you switched tongues, you had to remind yourself to switch to the other language. In which language did you remind yourself to do that? Did you think, say, in English that you needed to switch to Spanish (or vice versa)? My guess is that you didn't. You thought outside language. Try it again to see that you can think outside of language. Reiterate: *I am not my language.*

Looking into the Internal Mirror: I Am Not My Own Mind

You now stand in front of the final inner mirror, the mirror of consciousness. You've been looking for your essential self in all kinds of mirrors and, so far, you've found nothing. But you're closer than ever. You are almost home, in the doorway of your essential nature. Walk in. And since you're at home, it's time to strip down to your informational skivvies: time to root out this illusion that you are mind.

Let's drill down through the last layer of this informational onion, past all of our identification with our own thought contents. Let's scrub the mirror of consciousness clean. Once you learn to dis-identify from the internal stuff that you think you are, shedding the external identifications that bug you will be about as easy as turning on your windshield wipers. Heads up: so far in this chapter, we have been mowing the informational grass with the blades of neti-neti meditations and me/not-me checks. In this next section we will roll out the power tool of mindfulness meditation. The soil of your consciousness will never be the same after you plumb its informational depths with the plow of mindfulness. By learning how to step back from your thoughts, feelings, and sensations you will be severing the very root network of your false identities. After we work your mind over with mindfulness a bit, we will do another final weed clearing with the help of more neti-neti and me/not-me checks to make sure we didn't miss any stand-alone identity weeds.

---

the mind flows,
but we remain the same

Neti it out: *I am not my thoughts.*

My guess is that you've had millions of thoughts, and all of them have come and gone. The fact is, there has never been a thought that didn't go away. Sure, it might have lingered for a while; it might have even come back. But then it eventually passed on.

So, here are a few questions for you. Are we our thoughts? Do we become the thoughts that pass through us? Are *we* carried away with all this incessant mind-flow or do we somehow remain? To help you ponder this, here are a couple of quotations on the matter. Once you read them, these quotations will become your thoughts (at least while you're reading them). Ponder if—upon having these thoughts—you, yourself, have become these thoughts.

"If all of your experiences, your various states of consciousness, were weather patterns—clouds, rain, rainbows, tornados, hurricanes, or summer breezes—your consciousness would be the sky in which they take place. Your consciousness is the context in which all of your experiences, perceptions, thoughts, or feelings converge" (Schlitz, Vieten, and Amorok 2007, 17).

"Consciousness is the essence of the self" (Radhakrishnan and Moore 1957, 250).

Try this as well: have a thought, any thought, no matter how illogical or irrational, the kind of thought you'd never have. For example, run this thought through your mind: "I am Martha Stewart." Literally, run this thought through the ticker tape of your consciousness. And now ask yourself: am I now Martha Stewart or am I still me? Has this thought changed the essence of what I am, or have I remained essentially the same? Try this with any thought about yourself.

What have you concluded? And, more importantly, what have you concluded it *with*? Meditate on this. Conclude: *I am not my thoughts.*

Me/not-me check. Permanence question: Do you still go on after a thought passes through the field of your consciousness? Yes. When you change your mind, do you cease to exist? No. Do you have to keep thinking the same thought in order to continue to be your essential self? Doesn't seem so. Can you survive without your favorite thoughts about yourself? Of course. Recognize that your thoughts are not a permanent part of you. Conclude: *I am not any information that passes through me. I am not my mind forms.*

The Mind Is Information

Typically, we think of consciousness and mind as the same thing. They are not. *Mind* is information; that is, it's a particular form (pattern) of consciousness. *Consciousness* is what mind is made of. Consciousness is the substance of the mind, just like clay is the substance of a cup. The clay is the matter (essence), while the cup is the pattern (form). Consciousness, as the substance from which our thoughts, feelings, memories, and fantasies are made (formed), is constantly in transition, like wax in a lava lamp, changing from this to that. Mind is the particular form that this consciousness wax morphs into, the particular form (pattern) of consciousness. Thus, mind is *information*, and consciousness is *that* which is *in* formation, simultaneously arising and dissolving from a form to a form, from a pattern to a pattern.

By the same token, you aren't information; you are that which is in formation—the indefinable essence that manifests as thoughts, feelings, and sensations. In short, you aren't mind, you are the consciousness behind it. And to continue to identify with what you aren't is to continue to pollute what you are. Whereas ego identity is an identification with one's mind and its forms (thoughts, feelings, sensations), lotus identity is an identification with one's consciousness. To summarize:

1. Mind is information.

2. You are not information.

3. Therefore you are not mind.

So, without any further ado, lose your mind to find your consciousness. Clean the mind smudges off the mirror of your consciousness so that you can catch another glimpse of your essence.

the mind is a leg

Neti it out: *I am not my thinking act.*

When we were looking at the mirror of behavior earlier, we established that we are not what we do—that we are not our actions or our behavior. That was a relatively straightforward dis-identification to make. Now let's build on that. Mindfulness meditations show that the mind moves, just like the body. Rodolfo Llinas, a neuroscientist and author of *I of the Vortex: From Neurons to Self*, offers a framework that helps make sense of this movement (2002). Llinas proposes that mind is a kind of glorified movement system that has evolved to assist a multicellular organism with *motricity* (evasive action). The mind—for all intents and purposes—is the body, and thinking is action.

The gerundive word "being" says it all: life is motion; it's always in process, always in formation. Not coincidentally, the word "emotion," for example, is related to the word "motion." Indeed, we experience emotions as some kind of inner motion: first, you feel one way; then, all of a sudden, you are moved in another affective direction. The same goes for urges and impulses. Words themselves tell the story: impulse—from Latin *impulses,* meaning "push, shock, pressure"; urge—from Latin *urgere,* which means "to press hard" (www.etymonline.com). The mind streams, presses, pushes, shoves, acts out. Ever restless, it keeps you up at night. Notice the active tone in the advice of Swami Vivekananda: "Hold to the idea [that] 'I am watching my mind act,' and each day the identification of yourself with thought and feeling will grow less" (1993, 59).

You are not your mind act, you are not what your mind does, you are not your mind's movement; you are that changeless, motionless backdrop that allows you to observe all this internal commotion. You are not your outer behavior. You are not your inner behavior. You are not an act—physiological or mental. Conclude: *I am not my thoughts or feelings or sensations or memories or images. I am not my mind act.*

the mind fails the permanence criterion

Neti it out: *I am not form.*

Watch a lava lamp. If you don't have one, imagine it. See (imagine) the wax morph from one form to another. What you are watching is a flow of information. First, the wax inside the lamp is like this. Then, it's like that. So, how is the wax—like this or like that? Both and neither? Recognize that while the form mutates, the wax itself is immutable. Nothing changes about the essence of the wax itself despite all the changes of form that it is undergoing.

Meditate on the lava lamp inside your own head. Notice your thoughts arise, form, transform, and dissolve. Recognize that despite all this mind-stream, you, in your essence, stay the same. The constant ebb and flow of mind forms means that the mind fails the criterion of permanence to qualify as your essence. Conclude: *I am not the ebb and flow of my mind forms. I am not form. I am not mind.*

the mind fails the locality criterion

Neti it out: *I am not my own image of what I am.*

Recall that you are not a reflection in the physical mirror. Double check if you're not sure. You are not a reflection in your internal mirror either.

Close your eyes. Bring up an image of yourself. Recognize that in order for you to be seeing the image of yourself in your head, you have to be somehow separate from what you're seeing. If you are separate from the image you're seeing, then you are not the image of yourself (or any image in your head for that matter). An image is just one form of mind. If you are separate from one mind form, then chances are you are also separate from the rest of them (as the following exercises will demonstrate). To amplify this sense of dis-identification from the image, ask yourself: who is this who is seeing this mental reflection? Conclude: *I am not a mental reflection of who/what I am. I am not my mind.*

the apple of your "I"

Neti it out: *I am not an informational structure.*

Think of an apple. Imagine it, in all its details. Now, answer me this: is there an actual, physical apple inside your head? Of course not. This image of an apple you see is an informational structure. It's a representation of an object, not the object itself. Try to bite into it. You can't.

Now think of yourself. Recognize that this image that you have of yourself is also an informational structure, a tangle of cross-referenced associations, a mind form. You can no more bite into this apple of your "I" than you can bite into an imaginary apple. To "dial up" dis-identification, ask yourself: who is this who is thinking of one's self right now? Notice the information arise and dissolve. Notice that you remain, unaffected. Conclude: *I am not an informational structure. I am not a mind form.*

the essence of the mirror

Neti it out: *I am not what I reflect on.*

As you look at your reflection in the mirror, ask yourself: what makes a mirror a mirror? Recognize that the essence of the mirror is the capacity to reflect. And then ask yourself: what about me? What is my essence? Reflect on this question, on whatever information arises in response to it, and on whoever/whatever it is that is doing the reflecting. Conclude: *I am not what I reflect on. I am not the content of my reflection or thought processing. I am not an inner reflection. I am not my mind.*

anatomically internal = experientially external

Neti it out: *I am not my sensations.*

Take a sip of water mindfully. Witness the sensation of the sip. Ask the locality question: where is this sensation located in relation to its observer? Outside, of course. Anatomically inside, *but experientially outside* in relation to you-the-observer. Recognize that you are not that which you observe or experience. Conclude: *I am not this sensation. I am not any of my sensations.*

feel the feeling pass

Neti it out: *I am not my feelings.*

Mark Epstein, MD, a psychiatrist and the author of *Thoughts Without a Thinker: Psychotherapy from a Buddhist Perspective*, notes that "we instinctively identify with our emotional responses" and emphasizes the importance of "breaking identification" with our thoughts and feelings through "the power of awareness" (1995, 124-25). He's right: feelings are like tinted glasses in that they tone up or tone down our experience of reality. We tend to forget all about these emotional lenses through which we witness the world. So, let's spend a few minutes witnessing feelings themselves.

Think of an emotional splinter that got under your skin of late. Let yourself get fired up and then, as soon as you begin to feel it, pull back to watch this emotional drama arise and vanish. Notice the feeling come and go. Realize that here you still are. Recognize that there has never been a feeling that didn't eventually go away. What a relief to know that! Conclude: *I am not this feeling. I am not any feeling.*

space between "witness" and "it"

Neti it out: *I am not it.*

Notice the following phrase: "witness it." Notice the space between the word "witness" and the word "it." This space isn't just grammar. The space between the word "witness" and the word "it" parallels the geometry of observation. Without a space in between the witness and the object of observation, without the separation between the subject (the observer) and the object (of observation), there can be no witnessing.

Stand in front of a wall-mounted mirror. Notice the reflection of the tip of your nose. Notice the space between you and this reflection. Here you are, maybe a couple of feet away from the mirror, and there's the reflection of your nose, a couple of feet away from your nose. It is this space that allows you to witness this reflection. Now let's eliminate this space. Walk up to the mirror and press your nose into it. See the tip of your nose disappear. Recognize: no separateness, nothing to observe. Recognize: *if I am observing it, I am not it.* Recognize that this holds for both the external and the pseudo-internal (the *pseudo-internal* is that which is anatomically internal, such as a thought, but experientially external to the witness-you who is observing the thought). If you are having a mindless sip of water, you are the sip. If you are not mindfully there to observe it, there is no distance between you and the sensation. You are all body. You are all action. When, however, you turn your mind on, all of a sudden there is a distance, a space between you-as-observer and this internal object, this thought, this sensation, this feeling. Conclude: *I am not what I observe, notice, pay attention to, register, feel, sense, or think.*

Mindfulness as Dis-identification

Mindfulness is a dis-identification power tool. Contrary to how it sounds, mindfulness isn't about filling up your mind; it's about passively dis-identifying from your mind. "Passively" is the key word here. The neti-neti approach we've been using is an act of active dis-identification. Mindfulness is a letting-go kind of dis-identification, dis-identification by witnessing rather than by cutting off. Mindfulness is dis-identification by letting the mind come and letting it go. Mindfulness is the attitude of a doorway without a door: it notices the traffic but makes no effort to direct it. The following several exercises are variations on Vipassana-style mindfulness. Experiment with them. Practice them. Use them as dis-identification power tools.

sharpen the weeding blade of mindfulness: witnessing TV

Before you watch TV next time, try *witnessing* it. Turn the TV on and, on a piece of paper, mindfully, with consciousness, put down a dot each and every time a commercial comes on. Why? To step back from it. See, what often happens is that we get so plugged in to TV that we hardly even notice when the show breaks for commercial. We stay glued to the screen, regardless of what's on it. By marking down a dot each and every time a commercial comes on, you are popping out of the programming stream, and, if only for a moment, you become you, the witness of what is going on. This way you have an opportunity to re-enter yourself, to become a witness of your experience, as opposed to being drowned in it. When the commercial ends, mindfully, with a conscious sense of self-presence, put down another dot. Practice TV witnessing. It'll help you learn how to witness the built-in TV channel of your mind without taking it too seriously.

sharpen the weeding blade of mindfulness: watching the river

James Austin, neurologist, author of *Zen and the Brain*: *Toward an Understanding of Meditation and Consciousness,* called the mindful state of effortless witnessing a "riverbank attitude" (1999). Try it out. Watch your thoughts drift on by. Each and every time you recognize that you have a new thought event (mental image, sensation, or feeling), mark down a dot on a piece of paper with a pen or a pencil. Set an alarm clock for five minutes and watch your mind like this while marking down dots, one after another. Remain a dispassionate observer of whatever pops into your head, as if you were sitting on the bank of a river watching boats pass by. Just watch the mind flow, watch the thoughts come and pass down the river, staying where you are, in this riverbank attitude, without getting carried away downstream and without getting caught up in any particular thought. When the time is up, look at the dots on the paper. Realize that the thoughts came and went, but you're still here.

sharpen the weeding blade of mindfulness: watching the river (portable)

This is a more portable version of the river-watching meditation: instead of jotting down dots, rest one of your hands with its palm down on top of your knee and gently tap away the thoughts with your index finger. So, each and every time you witness your mind change, each and every time you notice a new thought, feeling, or sensation arrive onto the shores of your awareness, tap it away.

You may wonder what is up with all this jotting down dots and tapping. Here's my thinking on the matter. Each thought is the beginning of an action sequence. Each thought wants to graduate to a level of action, so to say. It carries an action/impulse potential. The tap (or the jotting down) discharges this action potential, grounding the impulse energy in a generic, nonspecific manner, thus completing the "life cycle" of a thought. The tap (or the dot) is a behavioral deflection. Most of the time when we witness the flow of our thoughts, we can just sit through it. But now and then something emotionally charged sneaks up on us, gets to us—and we bolt. We suddenly abandon the meditation session. I have found that this jotting/tapping element serves as an effective way to bolt without bolting, to act out the thought impulse without abandoning the meditation place. Use the tap instead of jotting down dots to make the exercise more publicly portable, less conspicuous.

sharpen the weeding blade of mindfulness: just sit and watch

After a couple of weeks of practicing the meditations above, try river-watching without either jotting down or tapping away the thoughts. Just sit and watch the mind flow. There's nothing to do, nowhere to go. You made time to be here, so be here. The world will wait. Remember that the whole business of jotting dots or tapping away thoughts is just training wheels on a bicycle. When you've learned to stay balanced and unperturbed by the passing thoughts, you can go for a ride without these assistive devices.

So, this has been a brief training in mindfulness. Of course, you'll be needing more practice using this power tool of dis-identification. You've got the rest of your life to hone this skill. In the meantime, let's return to our neti-neti/not this-not that clean-up operations as we get our consciousness ready for the seeds of lotus identity.

remain unstirred by recycled consciousness

Neti it out: *I am not my rumination.*
I am not my informational contents.

You might ask: "If these thoughts are so impermanent, then why do I keep thinking some of them? Why, for example, do I keep having the same thoughts about myself?" Let's see if I can explain. I'm sure you've had the experience of having a song stuck in your head. "There it is," you think to yourself, noting the intrusion into your consciousness. Author David Harp's concept of "recycled" consciousness can help make sense of these repetitive thought patterns (1996). Let's say you grew up in a hypercritical environment. As you matured, this cacophony of criticism taught you a jingle of self-deprecation. You've internalized the toxic noise of constant criticism, and these messages have become part of your own mind. While any of these thoughts of self-loathing are, indeed, impermanent, their recurrence creates a perception of permanence. In reality, however, they are nothing more than recycled consciousness on a feedback loop.

The mind is associative. Somebody criticizes you, and this triggers a train of thought, a chain of associations: before you know it you've got the jingle of self-loathing on playback. But then the thought passes, as all thoughts do. Internal associations may stir up this cognitive debris as well. So, what should you do about this junk in your head? Well, there is nothing that really needs to be done. By disputing this information directly, you are taking it seriously, giving it more airtime, so to speak. Do what you do when you notice a catchy tune in your mind: accept it for what it is—recognize that it's just a catchy jingle that doesn't mean anything.

Let's practice this attitude. Fill a glass with water. Get a tea bag and tear it open. Dump the loose tea into the glass. Stir it up. Watch the tea swirl. Accept that this process takes time. Notice the water itself as the last particle of the tea burns its kinetic energy before it touches down on the bottom of the glass. Realize that associative rumination is just like that. Recognize that you are not the informational debris that's swirling around your mind, that you are that medium of consciousness in which this rumination is happening. Conclude: *I am not my informational contents. I am not my rumination. I am not my associations.*

---

evict your "self"

Neti it out: *I am not what I think I am.*
I am not my definition of self.

Remember the "dots" exercise where you watched the river of mind? Each and every time you recognized a thought (a mental image, a feeling, or a sensation) that was passing through, you marked a dot. Let's build on that now. First, dictate the following series of questions on a recorder. "Who am I? Who is this? Who is this who is insisting that it's me? Who is this who is asking the question? Who is this who is thinking who this is? Who is doing this? Who is asking 'who is this?'" After each question, pause for ten seconds or so. Record the whole series of questions several times so that you have about ten minutes' worth of recording.

Now, get a notepad and a pen and listen to the recording you've made. As you hear the questions, don't answer them. Let each answer emerge on its own. Watch what the mind spits out, and each time your mind offers an answer, mark down a dot. Witness your mind try to define itself. Recognize these answer-thoughts, these self-definitions, as nothing more than thoughts passing through your mind. Recognize that a definition is not that which is being defined. Realize that description is not that which is being described. Understand that a name is not what is being named.

When done, look at the paper dotted with acts of self-definition. Recognize that your mind is a guest in this house of am-ness. It keeps trying to justify its stay through self-reference, by offering you informational definitions of itself. Let this informational "self" quote itself all it wants. It's a wasted effort. Evict this tenant of a self, with all its baggage. Be the house—an open house. Recognize: this self that you think you are, you are not. You are a different kind of self—a self without quotation marks. Conclude: *I am not my definitions of self. I am not my thoughts.*

---

this = that

Neti "this" out.

For this exercise, let's start with a bit of preparation. Sit down and place your hands on your lap, palms down. Tap the index finger of your dominant hand on your knee, ever so slightly. Do it a few times. Let's think of this little gesture as a farewell to a thought.

Now close your eyes and start watching the river of information that's flowing through you. Whatever passes, whatever you notice (anxiety, sadness, emptiness, images, breath, or anything), think "I am not this, I am not this" as you simultaneously and ever-so-slightly bid the passing thought on its way with a tap of your index finger. Play with this for five or so minutes. Recall that thoughts, feelings, sensations, images, and memories are, in fact, external in the sense that they are outside the observer self. I expressed this idea earlier as "anatomically internal but experientially external." By the same token, we can say that any of this that we call "this" is actually "that." The word "this" points to something that is close, right in front of us, whereas the word "that" points to something that is farther away. But any this (be it this thought or this feeling) is still a "that" in the sense that it is outside of us, external to the observer self. Even "this thought" is still over there, across that gap, across that space between the witness and the witnessed.

Now try the exercise again, but instead of saying to yourself "Not this, not this," try saying "Not that, not that." When you switch from "this" to "that," you may notice that you feel less identified with all that's passing through you. Notice the distance widen between you and all that information that is passing through you. Conclude: *Even this isn't this, let alone that.* Top it off with the all-inclusive: *I am not this, I am not that.*

personality camouflage

Neti it out: *I am not my traits. I am not my personality.*

Personality is usually understood as a set of characteristics or traits that distinguishes one person from another. Personality is information about you. You are not information. You are that which this information is about. Therefore, you are not your personality. You are not your traits. You are not your characteristics. Traits are your psychological contour, your emotional and relational shape, how you present and manifest, your form. You aren't your form. You are not your Myers-Briggs type. You are not your MMPI profile. Psychological parameters, specs of your cognition, motivation, behavior, and affect are merely descriptions of you. You are not a description. You are that which is being described. Sure, you might present as an extrovert or an introvert, as type A or type B, as a neurotic or a hysteric. These characteristics, of course, exist: there is no walking on the sand of form without leaving informational footprints behind. Sure, you have a style about you, a way about you, a response set, a mode of engagement, a pattern of reactivity, a presentation, a tone, a feel. Consider your personality as your informational signature.

No doubt you wear your psychology a certain way. But you are not what you wear. You are not your psychological disguise. You are not your personality mask. You might find it interesting that the word "personality" comes from the Latin word *persona*, which means a mask. No need to confuse the mask with the original face behind it. This mask, like all camouflage, has an adaptive function. If you have it, it must have helped you survive. If you feel safe enough now to take it off, do. If you can't, you can't. But even if this camouflage has become your second skin, even if you cannot take it off on demand, you can still know that it is but a layer, a psychological covering, a manner in which you manifest, a way others experience you, a conditioned role you play out on the stage of life. In other words, you don't have to strip all the way down to know that you have clothes on.

Case in point: say that you're using superglue as part of some home-improvement project. As tends to happen, you end up getting a little bit of it on your fingertips, and it sets. So, here you are, with a whitish layer of artificial skin on top of your natural skin. You try to wash it off. You scrub with steel wool and get a bit off. But no matter how hard you scrub, if you're going to keep the skin on that finger, some of the glue will have to remain. So, you let go.

Personality is just like that. You were working on a home-improvement project, mediating, negotiating, withdrawing, pacifying, caretaking, participating in the family, and trying to improve your home dynamics (or, at the very least, trying to survive them). In the process, you adopted a certain psychological modus operandi. And now it's stuck like superglue. So be it. What matters is that you are not your inter- or intrapersonal signature. To get some mileage out of this realization, try this:

Write down whatever you know about your personality in the following format: "I = (such and such)." For example: "I = an extrovert" or "I am an introvert" or "I = a neurotic." If you know your personality profile, write that down as well. For example: "I am INFP" (Myers-Briggs for "introverted, intuitive, feeling, perceiving"). Describe yourself fully: "I am a (such-and-such) person" as in "I = an angry person" or "I = a pleaser." Make sure that each description is a full "I am" statement.

Now, having catalogued all these known facets of your personality, go over each and every one of these statements and cross the sign of equality. So, if you wrote down your Myers-Briggs type as "I = INFP," now *decisively* cross out the identification equation sign: "I ≠ INFP." Voice this dis-identification out loud: *"I am not INFP. INFP is a way to describe my personality. I am not my personality. INFP is a description of me. I am not a description. I am that which is being described."*

Me/not-me check. Permanence question: Have you changed over the years? Have you become more this way, less that way, personality-wise? If so, conclude: *I am not how I am right now. Nor am I how I have been.*

---

why label the water you carry?

Neti it out: *I am not my zodiac sign.*

A zodiac sign is celestial GPS, a sort of sky coordinate of your birth. These signs are poetic and possibly informative. But you aren't an astrological time-space coordinate of your birth. The where and when of your birth is just information about you. You aren't information. You are that which this information is about. If this information is useful to you, use it (it's a free cosmos). But don't get caught up in the identity as such.

Try the following. Astrology is based on the principle of "as above, so below." Get your hand-held mirror and raise it over your head. Look up: what do you see? A reflection of you? Conclude: "As below, so above." If astrology has anything empirically true to say, then it has to abide by its own equation. If what is above = what is below, then what is below = what is above. If your personality is a reflection of the stars, then the stars are a reflection of your personality. If stars determine how you are, then, by the dialectics of this equation, you determine the stars. If so, why not name the entire starry sky after yourself? Isn't the true significance of the astrological equation that it is bi-directional? So, go ahead; name the entire sky after you—call it "Nameless." Recognize: you aren't the name of the star you were born under. You aren't a category from a celestial personality classification. In the postverbal, essence-focused rather than form-focused age of Aquarius, we are all water-carriers. If so, why label the water you carry? Conclude: *I am not my zodiac sign. I am not my space-time astrological coordinate.*

---

sweat out the small stuff
(and big stuff too)

Neti it out: *I am not my anxiety.*

You've heard the self-help dictum: "Don't sweat the small stuff" (Mantell 1988). Why not? Sweating is a process of purification and detoxification. Why not feel anxious when you feel anxious? Why roll the glue-stick of emotional suppression on your psychological pores, clogging up the system? Why not let the anxiety sweat itself out?

Anxiety is a feeling. You are not a feeling. Why should you hold on to anxiety? So, whether it's big stuff or small stuff that got your feelings triggered, there is no need to run from them. Remember that there is a space between you-the-observer and that which you observe. If your anxiety has escalated enough for you to notice it, welcome it as a wake-up call. As soon as you become aware of anxiety, you also become safe. How come? Recall that if you are aware of something, you are not that thing. That's the geometry of observation. To be aware of something, you have to be separate from it. If your anxiety has broken into your field of awareness, then it—along with its affective flood—has also, paradoxically, dug out a mote between itself and you. I repeat: if you are aware of a feeling or a thought, then you are instantly dis-engaged and dis-identified from it. The paradox is that the anxiety, along with a sense of threat, brings with it an opportunity for safety. It is exactly for this reason that anxious hypervigilance is akin to mindfulness. Both hypervigilance and mindfulness are an intensification of attention. Both anxious hyperscanning and mindful witnessing are states of attunement.

Welcome any future bouts of anxiety as an opportunity for awareness and presence. Anxiety, just like mindfulness, nails you to the floor of the present. Sure, it comes with some sweating, with some somatic activation. But so what? It's not the sweat, the heartbeat, or the rapid breathing that you really fear when you're anxious, but the *meaning* of all these somatic markers of anxiety. But what is meaning? Meaning is a thought, a mind form. You aren't a thought of meaning. So, as the lava lamp of your anxiety morphs from a somatic symptom to a cognitive symptom, follow its metamorphosis with awareness. Notice its sensory signature (rapid heartbeat, trembling, rapid breathing), notice its affective signature (fear), notice its cognitive signature (thoughts of this or that). And recognize your fundamental separateness from all this. In the matter of awakening, what difference does the tone of the alarm clock make? Sometimes you'll be awakened to the present by beauty, sometimes by anxiety. Welcome all these opportunities for mindfulness. Recognize that if you are aware of your anxiety, you are not that anxiety. Conclude: *I am not this feeling of anxiety.*

Me/not-me check. Permanence question: How many feelings have you been through in your life? Countless number. And yet, here you are. Recognize that feelings come and go and, as such, are not a permanent part of your essence. Conclude: *I am not my fleeting, transient, impermanent emotional states. I am not my feelings. I am not my anger, my anxiety, or my sadness. I am not my rage, my frustration, my surprise, or my shock. I am not my irritability, my boredom, or my fear.* Locality question: Where are these feelings? Anatomically, within the confines of your body. But what about in relation to the observer, to the one who is noticing these feelings? Somehow outside of the essential you that is noting these passing, fleeting, impermanent emotional states.

Conclude: *I am not what I observe, witness, note, or experience. I am not the emotional information that passes through. I am not my emotional responses.*

---

worry is science fiction. read it.

Neti it out: *I am not my worry.*

Worry is like anxiety minus somatic arousal. Worry is threatening thoughts about all that might happen in the future. It's scientific in its initial attempt at logic, starting with facts and escalating into fiction. Face it: the future doesn't yet exist. It hasn't happened yet. Nowhere in this universe does the future exist. Everyone and everything is right now, only now, ever now, never not now. Recognize that no matter how much you worry about the future, you will never experience it. The future doesn't exist. What exists is your thoughts about what doesn't exist. All you've ever experienced and will ever experience is a particular "now" that you're in.

With this in mind, sit back and bring up your frequent-flyer worries. Notice them arise. Notice them pass. Notice the one noticing. Is the one noticing worried? How can the observer self be worried by thoughts about the future when it, itself, is in the present? How can the observer self be worried by thoughts about one's future non-existence when it, itself, unambiguously exists in this very moment? Recognize that worry, too, is just information that is passing through you. Allow yourself to worry, notice the worry thoughts, and make a mental note: "Worry thought...another worry thought...worry thought again..." Tune in to the inevitable passing of these thoughts rather than to their informational content. Conclude: *I am not these worry thoughts. I am not my worry.*

Me/not-me check. Locality question: Where is this worry thought located, inside or outside? Inside. Inside what? Your mind. But where is this thought located in relation to you, the observer? Outside. Conclude: *I am not this worry thought.* Permanence question: Can you continue to exist without this thought? Will you cease to be when this thought passes through?

Recognize: here you are, before, during, and after this thought of worry. You—in your essence—remain the same: unaffected, immutable, witnessing and dis-identifying from what is passing. Lazily, unhurriedly, like an ocean waiting on a wave to fade out, like a lotus leaf waiting on a raindrop to roll off its luscious, invulnerable surface.

---

re-drawing the boundary

Neti out what no longer defines you.

Recall the exercise from chapter 2 in which you defined your "self" (Plant a Lotus Seed: Draw a Boundary). Let's revisit that. Find your original drawing. Look at what you have written down (with a pencil, I hope) inside the circle of self. Erase what no longer applies. Erase the information that you no longer consider to be inalienable to your essential self. Ponder what remains.

Consciousness Is Self-Cleaning

Suzuki (1956) reports the following curious exchange between Yun-men (a Zen master) and a fellow monk. When asked "Who is Buddha?" Yun-men said: "The dried-up dirt cleaner." To my analysis, this a rather profound response, although it doesn't seem so at first. After all, Buddha as a dirt cleaner? What does that mean? Let's take a look. But first, a word about the meaning of "buddha." There's nothing religious about this word—it simply means "awakened, aware" and originates from the Pali verb *budh*, meaning "to awaken" (www.ety-monline.com). Thus, the term "buddha nature" can be taken to mean animated nature, nature that is aware.

Buddha nature is consciousness. Here's the Dalai Lama equating buddha nature with consciousness: "This consciousness is the innermost subtle mind. We call it Buddha nature, the real source of all consciousness" (Gyatso 1988, 45). Indeed, consciousness, since it exists, is part of nature, and its defining characteristic is that it is aware. In fact, the two words "consciousness" and "awareness" are functionally interchangeable. So, what did Yun-men mean when he described Buddha as a dirt cleaner? Perhaps that buddha nature (consciousness) is self-cleaning. Recall the lava lamp once again. Within it there is wax (the substance, the essence) and then there are various forms that it takes (the information). The mind is made of consciousness, just like any given wax-form is made of wax. As the wax moves, it self-cleans: through constant movement, it continuously sheds one form after another. It is the very movement of the underlying wax substance that accounts for the arising and the cessation of any given form. It works the same way with consciousness: in its continuous, uninterrupted flow, consciousness cleans its own house— each thought, feeling, and sensation that emerges eventually passes. Consciousness is its own broom. It takes out its own mind-garbage. In its ceaseless flow, consciousness wipes its own slate clean time and again. Information ripples through consciousness like a wave across the ocean until it eventually fades out. Here's what Thich Nhat Hanh, a noted Buddhist thinker, says on this point in *Opening the Heart of the Cosmos: Insights on the Lotus Sutra*: "The wave does not have to seek to become water—she *is* water, right here and now. In the same way…you are already a Buddha" (Thich Nhat Hanh 2003, 81). If so—if consciousness, like water, is self-cleaning—then why should you bother with an identity (informational) detox if there's never been a thought that didn't go away? The idea here is to help the process along, to tone down the informational tsunami, to learn to surf the mind-waves without drowning.

the placid lake of consciousness

Neti it out: *I am not what comes over me.*

Sometimes we feel that something comes over us. The mind changes, and we feel that we change too. But do we?

Fill a glass with water. Wait until the water settles, then stir it up with your finger. Watch the waves of the vortex warp the surface. Now sit back and watch the water clean itself of all these wave forms. What you are witnessing is a process of self-cleaning. Recognize that your consciousness works the same way. Notice that while it certainly takes time for informational ripples to fade out, they always do. Recognize that no matter what you've ruminated over or worried about in your life, no matter how long that song was stuck in your head, eventually all those thoughts (images, feelings, sensations, or memories) dissolved back into the surface of your consciousness. Indeed, there has never been a thought (mind form) that didn't go away. Knowing this, recognize that you don't have to be afraid of your mind forms any more than a lake has to fear the waves on its surface or the lotus has to fear the morning dew. Conclude: *I am not what comes over me. I am not my mind.*

Me/not-me check. Permanence question: Are you your emotional states or what precedes them and remains after they pass? Are you these passing, fading, dissolving informational ripples through your consciousness or that which remains? Ponder this and, hopefully, conclude: *I am not my informational states.*

write on your consciousness

Neti it out: *I am not my fixations.*

Find the largest pan or pot you have and fill it up with water. Now write your name on the surface of the water. What happens? The writing dissolves instantaneously. Try it again. Can you even get past the first letter? Not really. Water is too fluid to hold form. Now, imagine that you filled this pan with thick honey. Chances are that your name would keep its form for a while but would eventually smooth out. Fluidity is self-cleaning. Consciousness is just like that. If you watch the river of your consciousness closely, you will notice a constant arising and cessation of various mind forms. Each passing of a thought owes to the self-cleaning nature of consciousness.

Try writing on your consciousness. Close your eyes and try to hold on to a thought of your choice. Notice how difficult it is: as soon as you think the thought, your consciousness bucks like a wild horse, as if to shrug off the thought that artificially constrains it. Notice how, despite your best efforts, the target thought keeps getting interrupted by other thoughts. If you were to persist with this for a few minutes, you would probably eventually feel like you'd been in a batting cage, with interfering thoughts constantly whizzing into and out of your consciousness. Consciousness, just like water, is too fluid to freeze in any given mind form. Like water, it's self-cleaning. Lotus-like, consciousness repels the information. That's why you've never had a thought that didn't go away.

If you're wondering about rumination, obsessing, dwelling, and "songs" that get stuck in your mind, hold tight: we'll come back to this illusion of permanence a little later in the book. Conclude: *I am not my mental fixation or obsessions. I am not what I ruminate about. I am not my mind patterns. I am not my mind.*

dumping the informational ballast

Neti out perfectionistic desires to neti out everything.

You don't have to be a perfect Buddha about dis-identifying from all this information about you. Dis-identify only from the information that weighs you down. Dump the informational ballast. That's enough.

To see what I mean, try this: Get out your hand-held mirror. Paint it over with watercolors. Entirely cover the surface of the mirror, then wait until the paint dries up. Now look at the front of your mirror. Notice that the reflection is gone. Now that the surface is matte, the mirror doesn't work. Recognize this as a metaphor of your old, ego-based self. Covered with information, you couldn't see yourself.

In the course of this informational detox, you have been cleaning and polishing the mirror of your consciousness. But it's quite all right if the mirror isn't perfectly clean. You don't have to clean the entire mirror to use it. So go ahead and wipe off a portion of the hand-held mirror. Only clean a portion. See? While not completely clean, the mirror already works. My point is this: dump the identities that weigh you down. That's enough. If you feel like going all the way and being a perfect Buddha, you can—you've got the rest of your life to work on this process. But for now, recognize that as long as you have a point of access to your essential sense of self, as long as you have a way in, you've got all you need in order to grow. You've treaded the path. And now you know how to get back home when you need to. Case in point: I've been in this country for twenty years. I used to be self-conscious about my accent. Then I realized: I am not my accent. I dis-identified from it. Later, I noticed that my accent would get worse whenever I felt anxious. So, I dis-identified from my anxiety about my accent. Indeed, I'm not my anxiety about my accent. I am not a feeling that I have about the sound of my voice. Eventually, I noticed that sometimes I'd have anxiety about the possibility of being anxious about my accent. So, I dis-identified from that too. I am not my worry about becoming anxious about my accent getting worse should I get anxious. Gradually, my accent improved. I kind of like it now. To tell the truth, I now identify with it a bit. Yep, I am not a perfect Buddha. Even if I were, I wouldn't be. That's the nature of the mirror. The reflection is both a part of the mirror and apart from the mirror. The mirror is both the reflection that it is and, at the same time, not the reflection that it is. Form is not essence and essence isn't form. And yet, there is no essence without form and there is no form without essence. The historical Buddha said as much: form is emptiness, emptiness is form. This = that. So, why identify with either? I don't identify with my attempts to dis-identify. And neither should you. Conclude: *I am not my lotus effect. I am not my growth. I am not my attempts at self-help. I am not my meditation practice.*

the hard problem of consciousness made a bit easier

Neti it out: *I am not my brain chemistry.*

You've probably heard this notion expressed time and again: consciousness is a function of your brain's neurochemistry; in other words, you are your brain chemistry. This is really curious, isn't it? How do we draw a line of equation between chemistry and psychology, between inanimate molecules that are being passed around inside the neural labyrinth of our brain and our experience? With the word "function"?

The question I am posing here is known as the "hard problem of consciousness." Here's how it has been formulated by author T. H. Huxley (1868, 178): "[H]ow is it that any thing so remarkable as a state of consciousness comes about as the result of irritating nervous tissue?" Here's how David Chalmers (1995, 200-219) re-introduced this problem into the philosophical discourse in the mid-nineties: "Why should physical processing give rise to a rich inner life at all?"

Imagine the following. You are microscopically small and you go on a tour of somebody else's brain. So, here you stand, on the edge of a synaptic gap the size of the Grand Canyon. Your tour guide (just as small as you are) informs you that in a moment you will witness an act of neural transmission. And, indeed, in a moment you witness a massive discharge of gigantic neurotransmitter molecules from one edge of the canyon. These molecules head across the synaptic abyss, toward the other side. Some of these giant molecules are taken into the cliff side of the other neuron, whereas others float around in the gap between the neuronal cliffs and are eventually reabsorbed by the cliff that had originally discharged them (the pre-synaptic neuron).

After checking his walkie-talkie, your tour guide explains: "Those were endorphins. The owner of this brain just got off the treadmill and is about to have a feeling of euphoria." "Excuse me," you cut in, "Who owns this brain? And where will the owner of this brain experience the euphoria?" "Come, I'll show you," says the guide, and the two of you transport to a different part of the brain. The guide points to a particular area and says: "Truth be told, we don't really know where the owner of the brain is. We think the brain may be its own owner. We think it is self-governed. One thing we do know is that this part right here is very important. We call it the 'frontal lobe' because it's anatomically in front of the brain and appears to be functionally in a position of leadership. It's responsible for the so-called 'executive' functions. It's like the CEO of the brain. Do you wish to take a closer look?"

As you agree, the two of you descend the already-familiar landscape of the giant neuronal fjords. As before, all you see is synaptic cliffs and hordes of molecules being passed around across the synaptic gaps. "So where's this CEO, this self you alluded to?" you ask. "There," says the guide, pointing at a bunch of chemical cliffs. "Hmm," you mutter to yourself, perplexed. "What about that euphoria you mentioned?" The tour guide whisks you over to another part of the brain. "We call this region the limbic circuit. This is part of the emotional brain. We suspect this is where the feeling of endorphin-triggered euphoria is being processed." As you survey the limbic system, you find the same picture as before: synaptic cliffs and molecules being transported across the synaptic divide, some of which linger for a while and get re-absorbed into the pre-synaptic cliffs, only to be released later. You pick up a couple of smaller molecules that are lying around. As you toss these chemical marbles from one hand to another, you wonder how this mechanical action of moving a material (physical, chemical) object from one location (one hand, one neuron) to another location (another hand, another neuron) results in a conscious experience. Not having much hope for clarity, you nevertheless ask: "Sir, we've been all around this brain. All we've seen is neurons transporting chemicals across synaptic gaps. We haven't seen the owner of the brain. We haven't seen any feelings. All we've seen is chemistry, physics, matter. Can you explain how all this physico-chemical hardware produces the psychology of my experience?" "Oh, that," exclaims the tour guide, beaming. "That's quite simple. The psychology of your conscious experience is a *function* of your brain chemistry. Get it? Anyway, tour's over. Time to go."

So, here you are. You've been introduced to the hard problem of consciousness, and you've imagined it. What's left is to imagine how a material reaction translates into consciousness. It may seem unimaginable to you. Indeed, how does chemistry produce psychology? How does the brain (a material structure) produce the mind (an informational structure)? You've also got the answer: you—the very you that you are experiencing right now as your sense of self—is nothing but a *function* of your brain chemistry, a *product* of the chemical domino effect, a *consequence* of matter.

What you're being asked to accept is literally this: *mind* = *brain* or *psychology* = *chemistry/physics* or *body* = *mind* or *consciousness* = *matter*. Sounds strange when stated like this, huh? What we usually hear is that "consciousness is a function of brain chemistry." The word "function" infuses some kind of mediation magic into this equation; it buffers the impact. But the word "function" is just a word of causality. To say that event B is a function of event A is to say that event A caused B. When we say that consciousness (event B) is the function of brain chemistry (event A), we are saying that brain chemistry causes/ creates consciousness. In other words, chemistry creates psychology.

If you were to take a lump of clay and create a cup, you are shaping clay into a particular form. The resultant form, the cup, is still made of clay. By the same token, when you take a handful of chemistry and shape it into some psychology (the mind, experience), the resultant psychology is made of chemistry. In other words, when you are told that your consciousness is a function of brain chemistry, you are being told that you are literally chemistry, that your consciousness is matter.

I agree. Consciousness *is* matter and matter *is* consciousness. That's exactly why when you pop a pill (a material intervention) your consciousness changes. And that's why when you think new thoughts (an intervention of consciousness) your brain chemistry changes. That's called neural plasticity. "What happens in your mind changes your brain, both temporarily and in lasting ways," explain Dr. Rick Hanson, a neuropsychologist, and Dr. Richard Mendius, a neurologist, in their book *Buddha's Brain* adding that "you can change your mind to change your brain to benefit your mind" (2009, 18). Consciousness is as much a function of your brain chemistry as your brain chemistry is a function of your consciousness.

But then, why identify with the material/chemical/structural side of this equation? Indeed, if you are both brain chemistry and consciousness, if the two are interchangeable, then why not dis-identify from the reductionist terminology of chemistry? Recognize that "I am a product of brain chemistry" is just another thought passing through your field of awareness. Conclude: *I am not brain chemistry. I am not my favorite theory of mind. I am not my favorite explanation of consciousness.*

conclusion: you are what remains

In trying to answer the question of "Who/what am I?" you've been searching outside of yourself—in physical mirrors, in the mirrors of others' minds, in social feedback, in public opinion, in your life circumstance, in your relational status or role, and in your material possessions. You've been also searching within—in your thoughts and feelings about yourself, in your self-definitions, in language, and in the mirror of time and bio-data. Here's what you have concluded:

* I am not a reflection in the physical mirror.

- I am not others' thoughts, others' reactions to me, or their expectations of me.

- I am not my own mind or the contents of my consciousness.

- I am not my own thoughts, feelings, sensations, or memories.

- I am not language, or any of the conceptual definitions of myself, or self-description of any kind.

- I am not the word "I" or any other words, my name, or my narrative.

- I am not any one moment in time.

- I am not my past, my accomplishments, my facts, or my history.

- I am not my potential or my future.

- I am not my social context.

- I am not what I have, what I make, or what I own.

- I am not my relational status or my roles.

- I am not my body, my age, my weight, or my appearance.

- I am not any of this.

- I am neither this nor that.

In short, you have concluded that *you are not the information about you.* Having looked into every possible informational mirror, all you've found is what you are not. You have found that you are not quantifiable or qualifiable. You've found that there isn't a mirror big enough or deep enough or accurate enough to reflect what you are. You have discovered that you are beyond reflection, beyond description, and beyond comparison. So, if you are none of this, then what are you? Indeed, that is the question.

"What am I?" Is this even an answerable question? Probably not in any kind of verbal, informational manner. If I ask you to point at the moon and you point randomly at the sky, we've got two issues. One: your directions are poor. Two: your directions—even if they were accurate—still wouldn't be the moon. Even a finger that precisely points at the moon still isn't the moon. Self-descriptions are verbal directions. Some are in the ballpark, some are off the chart. But even the most verbally precise self-descriptions are still just descriptions. And we are not descriptions of ourselves. And yet, descriptions (verbal directions) are useful. It sure helps to have a description that is at least in the verbal ballpark of what it purports to point to. Here's one such verbal pointer: "Consciousness is the essence of the self" (Radhakrishnan and Moore 1957, 250). Of course, your essence isn't the word "consciousness" itself; but if you are looking for a way to express who you are, you get closer to the truth by saying that you are your consciousness than by saying that you are your mind.

Here's another way to answer the question of "Who am I?" *You are not information, you are that which is in (the process of) formation.* Not a form, but that which is in the process of continuous formation. More of a verb than a noun. More the *am-ness* of the "I am" than the informational *I-ness* of it. After all, a verb is a part of speech that expresses the act of being, not its form or consequence. You are a *process* in formation, not any given informational outcome. The life itself. A being—part verb, part noun. Another way to answer the question of "What/who am I?" is to say that *you are that which remains* after you have exhausted all your attempts to define yourself. An emptiness? A nothing? No, not a nothing. Just something indescribable.

"But what is *that*?" you might still insist. You could answer this question the way Ken Wilber, an influential American philosopher, does by saying that you are "what remains," after you have asked yourself repeatedly "What am I?" and have dis-identified from all the false answers. As Wilber puts it, you are "a pure center of awareness, an unmoved witness of all these thoughts, emotions, feelings, and desires" (1998, 37). Or, perhaps the most elegant way to answer this question is to leave it open. But worry not: I neither possess the courage of such elegance nor think you would tolerate it. So, as you continue into the following chapters you'll explore ways to directly experience whatever it is that you are. Just remember that this process is not about coming to a set definition—it's about learning to dis-identify from what you are not and identify with that indescribable essence that you are.

You've walked a very long route, knocked on every door, and found no one of permanence inside. To bring this realization to the level of an actual lotus effect you will have to tread this informational obstacle course time and again until you learn how to walk past all these doors of identification without bothering to knock. To leverage lotus-like flow of undistracted growth, you will have to keep coming back to these ideas each time you stumble over a lump of informational dirt. It may sound difficult, but it really isn't. There's no need for miracles here, just a self-reinforcing practice of self-cleaning. I'm confident that once you get the hang of this dis-identify/re-identify business, you'll be doing it with gusto. After all, who wants to keep lugging all this informational baggage around?

Here's what I predict will happen. As you learn to reliably re-identify with whatever it is that you really are, your neural plasticity will come to the rescue. *Neural plasticity* is when you change your brain by changing your mind. By practicing to dis-identify from what you are not and re-identify with what you are, you will lay the neural rails for your future mind to run on. You will develop a habit of self-remembering, a habit of remembering that changeless, permanent sense of self that has been shadowing you through all your moments of mindfulness. And habits, after all, are second nature. So, as you keep at it (and I'll give you some ideas on how to further potentiate your lotus effect at the end of the book), it will become as natural as washing your face.

CHAPTER 4

not a nothing

[Sunyata doctrine] implies emptiness of inherent existence or own-being [essence]... Needless to say, emptiness is not to be confused with sheer nothingness or total blankness. Buddhism knows no ultimate vacuum...Tathagata-garbha doctrine, meanwhile, puts forward the notion that we are all in a sense wombs in which the seeds of Buddhahood can germinate.

John Snelling

Having planted the lotus seeds, having weeded out false identifications, having cleared out the soil of your consciousness, we now need to protect your budding lotus identity from the scorching shine of the Sunyata doctrine of "no self." Sunyata, in Sanskrit, means "emptiness, void." Here's how this doctrine is described by Buddhist scholars Samuel Bercholz and Sherab Chodzin Kohn: "Ancient Buddhism recognized that all composite things are empty, impermanent, devoid of essence, and characterized by suffering... [Sunyata] does not mean that things do not exist but rather that they are nothing besides appearances" (1997, 325). Feel the burn?

If all is devoid of essence, then do we even have a self? At a glance, the Buddhist answer would seem to be an emphatic no. Sunyata doctrine teaches that there is no such thing as a permanent self, that self, as an entity, is an illusion, leaving us to conclude that we don't really exist, that we are "nothing" but an "appearance." Worry not: you exist! I have a path in mind for sorting through this thorny issue. So, put your sunblock on and let's do some defensive gardening.

if you are reading this, you exist

Whenever you read Buddhism-inspired self-help literature, you run into a curious dilemma. On one hand, Buddhist psychology posits that there is no self; on the other hand, it offers various programs of self-help. This seeming contradiction makes me wonder three things:

- If there is no "self," then why is the author getting paid for the self-help book he did not write (because how can you write a book if there is no "self" to write it)?

- If there is no "self," then who is reading all these self-help books?

- If there is no "self," then what is the point of a self-help book?

Sounds like a paradox, doesn't it? It actually isn't. Buddhism does not deny the reality of your existence, it just encourages you to dis-identify from your informational self. But, in doing so, pop-Buddhism throws the baby of essence out with the informational bathwater. Indeed, after you strip away all the layers of your informational self, after you dis-identify from everything you are not, it can be all too tempting to conclude that since there is no fixed informational self, then you are a nothing, an emptiness. This, too, you are not. Here is Ken Keyes, Jr., the author of *Handbook to Higher Consciousness*, on this topic:

You watch your body and mind perform an ever-changing scenario of thoughts, feelings, sensations, and actions. You realize that you have no fixed self or fixed individuality that remains intact. Your name and your ego-based memory no longer give you the illusion of being an "individual." As you grow in consciousness towards the higher levels, you no longer identify the essence of you with your body, your worldly status, your programming, or your rational mind-stuff. You deeply experience your essence as being pure Conscious-awareness that just watches the drama of your life as it is acted out on the myriad stages of the world. (1975, 167-68)

Since this very question of whether there is or isn't a self comes with a good bit of existential tension, let me preview the conclusion of this discussion first and lay out the argument later. You are not a nothing. You are not an emptiness. The goal of this chapter is to neti out this toxic nihilism.

review: your mind is information, and you aren't your mind

Recall a point from earlier in the book: mind is the manifestation of consciousness. Mind is information; that is, particular form (pattern) of consciousness. Consciousness is what mind is made of. Consciousness is the stuff (substance) of the mind, just like clay is the stuff (substance) of a cup. Clay is the matter (essence). The cup is the pattern (form).

Consciousness, as the substance from which our thoughts, feelings, sensations, and memories are made (formed), is constantly in formation, like wax in a lava lamp, changing from *this* to *that*, from this mind form to that mind form. What we've been busy weeding out is the notion that you are this or that mind form. We established that you are not your mind, that you are not the form of your consciousness. In so doing, you have left yourself nothing informationally tangible to call your self. After all, "essence" does sound dangerously close to the idea of nothing. But you are not a nothing. A mirror doesn't stop being a mirror just because the light is off.

---

water the lotus seed:
see past the reflection to the mirror

Neti out the notion that you are a nothing.

Get a hand-held mirror. Stand in front of a wall with some pictures or shelves behind you. Look at the mirror. Notice how the entire mirror is covered with reflection. Every point of the mirror reflects something. The surface of the mirror is one big picture made up of the reflection of your face and of the objects around you. Notice that the objects immediately behind you aren't reflected in the mirror, as they are obscured by you. Now, holding the mirror still, move your head to the side and notice how the mirror immediately fills up with the reflection of what was behind your head. As always, there is no part of the reflecting surface of the mirror that doesn't reflect what's in front of it. Parts of the wall that were previously obscured are now reflected.

Recognize that, as long as there is light, the mirror will always be covered with reflection. See how this constant flow of reflections obscures the mirror. The mirror is always there, but we don't see the actual mirror, we see the reflections in the mirror. Recognizing this, now face the mirror, not its reflections. Look at the mirror and allow yourself to appreciate that you are looking both at the reflection and at the mirror itself. Spend some time in front of the mirror with this thought. Ponder how the mind obscures consciousness the same way the reflection in the mirror obscures the actual mirror. Recognize the invisible consciousness behind your own mind. It is like this mirror. Recognize that just because you cannot see the mirror behind the reflection doesn't mean that the mirror doesn't exist. Conclude: *I am not a nothing.*

water the lotus seed:
the untouchable and immutable
reality of you

Neti out the notion that you are an emptiness.

Get your hand-held mirror and go into a room that you can make really dark (like a bathroom or a closet), or have a thick blanket at the ready. First, with the light on, look in the mirror and see the reflection there. Now keep holding the mirror but turn off the light, close the door, or pull the blanket over your head. You don't see the reflection and you don't see the mirror. If the room is truly dark, there is no reflection on the mirror. The reflection disappeared. But the mirror didn't. Even though you don't see the mirror, it still exists. Touch it. There it is, the surface of the mirror. By way of touch, your hand is giving you a representation of the mirror that you had been relying on your eyes for. Functionally, the hand became the "eyes." We don't see through the eyes, we see through the mind's eye that is fed by whatever senses are available to us. In the absence of sight, the mind uses other senses to create an image or conceptual representation of reality, which it then sees.

Now move your hand away from the mirror (or, if you're using a hand-held mirror, put it down). Since the mirror doesn't smell or make sounds, you can't experientially establish that it exists without your sense of vision or touch. You know that it's there, in the darkness, but unless you are engaging it with your senses, you can't really experience it. Ponder this and recognize that it's the same with consciousness. You can't touch, smell, hear, or taste your consciousness, and that's why it's indescribable.

When you're in those gaps between thoughts, you know that you-as-consciousness, you-as-awareness, do exist. You *know* you exist. You don't need the evidence of your mind to verify your existence. You don't need the thought that you are perfect or the thought that you are valuable or any other self-evaluation or self-definition thought to know that you exist. Your existence is self-evident. Even when you are totally blank (whether in meditation or upon awakening or when shocked), you are aware of your own presence. There's no way to describe it, but it's real. We can call it emptiness, but it's not really that. It's *like* emptiness because it has no information in it, but it's different from emptiness because it's not a true absence. On the contrary, it's a presence, a presence of something that cannot be experienced with the senses.

Recognize that you-as-consciousness are untouchable and, therefore, invulnerable. Understand that because you are beyond description, you-as-consciousness cannot be evaluated, measured, ranked, or objectified. Recognize your essential freedom from evaluation! With nothing to evaluate, what is there to reject? With nothing to reject, you have no choice but to accept the real you! You can only reject your mind, but you cannot reject your consciousness. Think about this. Conclude: *I am not an emptiness.*

---

the absence of a fixed self doesn't mean an absence of a fluid self

The Eastern/Buddhist doctrine of "no self" (the notion that there is no essence or fixed self) offers an unnecessarily nihilistic spin on what's going on in your head: "Search as hard as we will, we can never point to anything in ourselves that we can definitely say is the self" (Snelling 1991, 53). Sounds like there is no self inside, doesn't it? But not exactly: there is a *self*, just not the kind of self that we thought. True, mindfulness meditation makes a convincing case for a lack of a *fixed* self. Neither thoughts nor feelings can constitute a permanent self (Snelling 1991) because thoughts and feelings are always in a state of flux, ever fleeting. This makes sense: just as we don't define the tree by its leaves (because they come and go with each season), we cannot define ourselves by the ever-changing objects of our consciousness (thoughts, feelings, sensations, and memories). Does this sound familiar? It's exactly what we were exploring in the preceding chapter. Indeed, information is too impermanent to be a foundation for a fixed self.

But the lack of a fixed self isn't necessarily proof of the absence of a fluid self. You see, Sunyata-style Buddhism, having failed to find the permanence of mind, has foreclosed on the permanence of the underlying consciousness. Just because you can't anchor your identity in your mind doesn't mean that you cannot identify with your consciousness. Just because the reflection on the mirror keeps changing doesn't mean that the mirror itself doesn't exist. In dis-identifying from the informational weeds of the mind, we don't have to scorch the soil of consciousness itself. A state of no-mind is still a state of consciousness. You are still there, even if you're in a state of informational silence. Realize that while the word "nothingness" exists, what it refers to doesn't. You cannot be an emptiness or a nothingness because, for either emptiness or nothingness to be more than just words, they would have to exist; that is, they would have to be some kind of something.

---

water the lotus seed:
buffeted by the stream of life

Neti out the notion that you don't exist
just because you can't hold form.

Get a long shoestring. Let's agree to call this shoestring your consciousness. Now, try to form the first letter of your first name with the string.

What you've just done is created information that symbolizes a fixed identity, a fixed informational self. Now, pull one of the ends of the shoestring to undo this informationally fixed structure. Information disappeared, but the shoestring is still there. Next, open your kitchen faucet and run some water. Make sure the stream is pretty strong. Hold the string in a manner that puts most of its length into the current of water. Let's agree that this current is the stream of life (the external sensory input). Notice the shoestring constantly move under the continuous pressure of this life stream. Notice the continuous transformation of its form. What you have here is a representation of life stream affecting the stream of your consciousness. Sometimes the string moves this way, sometimes it moves that way. The constant change in the string's movement, the impermanence of its form, does not in any way negate the fact of this string's existence.

It's the same way with you. You exist (while you do). While you exist, you are in constant flux, in a constant process of formation. But just because you are not a fixed informational pattern doesn't mean that your am-ness, your sense of self-presence, does not run through your life like a red thread. It does! Recognize that the impermanence of your mind does not negate the permanence of your consciousness.

a mash-up of two doctrines

The Sunyata doctrine of no self is balanced by the Buddhist doctrine of *Tathagatagarbha*. Very briefly stated, this doctrine posits that there is, within us all, Buddha nature, or the so-called "Buddhic self." To further understand what is meant by the term "Buddha nature," or "Buddhic self," recall that the word *buddha* simply means "awakened, aware." Thus, the term "buddha nature" can be taken to mean animated nature, nature that is aware—consciousness. So, these two doctrines, the Sunyata and the Tathagatagarbha, are basically two sides of the same coin. The Sunyata teaching says: we are not mind. Tathagatagarbha, in its secular reading, says: we are consciousness. Exactly! We aren't information, we are that which is in (the constant process of) formation. We aren't the reflection on the mirror, we are the mirror itself; not any of the objects of awareness, but the awareness itself. Not this or that form of the wax in the lava lamp, but the ever-transforming wax of our existence. We are not information, but the experiential point of view that experiences this information. An immutable *field of awareness*, not the fleeting informational contents within it. A *space that is aware*, as they say in Dzogchen Buddhism.

Examine the following words by Jack Kornfield from his wonderful book *After the Ecstasy, the Laundry*: "We usually take ourselves to be the sum of these thoughts, ideas, emotions, and body sensations, but there is nothing solid to them… Perhaps we can take a step back and look who it is that knows this, the space of knowing in which they arise" (2000, 74). So, we are "the space of knowing" in which we—our informational selves, our egos, our notions of self—arise. Professor Jeffrey Hopkins, in explaining the Tathagatagarbha doctrine, likens this Buddhic self (Buddha nature, also known as "Buddha matrix") to a hidden treasure that needs not be created anew but is merely in need of an informational detox: "An unknown treasure exists under the home of a poor person that must be uncovered through removing obstructive dirt, yielding the treasure that always was there" (2006, 9). Thus, the Sunyata doctrine can be understood as the *dis-identification arm* of our informational-detox formula, the broom that cleans out the informational clutter and frees up the "space of knowing" that you are, while the Tathatagarbha doctrine is the *re-identification arm* of this overall process of affirming your true, essential self—your Buddhic self, your lotus self.

emptiness as background, as the ground of being

Chogyal Namkhai Norbu, a renowned Dzogchen teacher, speaks of emptiness as our fundamental dimension and praises its utility: "In emptiness we start to be able to distinguish thoughts, movements, and manifestations" (2006, 112). Francesca Fremantle, in her book *Luminous Emptiness: Understanding the Tibetan Book of the Dead*, writes: "Emptiness is the heart of Buddhism...It is not negative. It is the creative source of all apparent existence... Emptiness is not simply a void that is left when illusions have been cleared away... it is a continuous process, the living essence of each moment of experience" (2001, 39).

When, after dis-identifying from everything we are not, we find the emptiness of no-self, what we are actually finding is the blankness of the page that allows us to see the text of our own self-narrative. Consciousness, spirit, essence, void, and emptiness are different words for one and the same thing-less-ness that we are. This emptiness that we find is our essential self, our Buddha nature, our consciousness. It is exactly on this ground of our being that all these different mind forms take root.

---

root of life

Neti it out: *I am not a nothing.*

In this exercise, we're working with a familiar neti in a different context to gain some additional insight. Get a blank piece of paper. Draw a tree. Label this tree "self." Note the quotation marks. Now, flip the paper over and write the word self without quotation marks. Recognize that the informational "self" that you've been thinking you are couldn't be possible without the actual self that you are. Recognize that it is the blankness of this page that is the root of the drawing on the other side. The tree of "self" you drew would have no ground to stand on if this page hadn't been blank.

Recognize that blankness isn't a nothing. A blank page of consciousness still exists. If it didn't, there would be no room for your mind drawings. Recognize that informational emptiness is not a structural emptiness. A tabula rasa is still a tabula, even if it's rasa. Conclude: *I am not a nothing!*

---

selflessness as false self

Peter Fenner, a former Buddhist monk with a doctorate in the philosophical psychology of Mahayana Buddhism, offers the following rebuke to Sunyata doctrine: "One of the most sophisticated ways of perpetuating the ego is found in the Buddhist theory of egolessness… The theory holds that we possess no solid core…thus, within this theory, the ego denies its own existence, and thereby creates the ideal and goal of realizing egolessness… The game plan of the ego goes undetected" (2002, 83). U. G. Krishnamurti expresses this idea with his characteristic directness: "Man is always selfish, and he will remain selfish as long as he practices selflessness as a virtue" (2002a, 110). Ken Wilber calls attention to this very point as well, calling on us to "better understand the real meaning of 'egolessness,' a notion that has caused an inordinate amount of confusion" (1998, 31). He clarifies: "Egolessness does not mean the absence of a functional self (that's psychotic, not a sage); it means that one is no longer exclusively identified with that self" (31).

As you see, the potential danger of misreading the Sunyata doctrine is that a pursuit of "no self" might insidiously turn into the pursuit of righteous selflessness (which also is ego) and into denials of one's motives. Having a motive isn't evidence of ego, it's just a vital sign of your being alive. Motivation is our life force, the source of our movements and flow. Motivation is what moves us; thus the semantic connection between these two words (moto-, motion, motivation). Motivation is nothing other than our inevitable pursuit of well-being. Motivation is part of our humanity. Motivation is what causes us to choose and act. It's just as inevitable as cause and effect. And yet for some of us motivation has come to mean selfishness. We see selflessness as an ideal and identify with it. Bottom line: own your motive, or risk having another false self. But don't just take my word for it. Let's learn from the "sacred lotus" itself.

It is 1996. Two physiologists, Dr. Roger S. Seymour and Dr. Paul Schultze-Motel, are studying the "heat of Nelumbo," the bizarre fact that *Nelumbo nucifera*, the sacred lotus, is capable of *thermogenesis* (the ability to self-regulate temperature within a certain range). In particular, they show that the lotus flower is capable of maintaining a temperature of between 86 and 95 degrees Fahrenheit, even when the temperature in its environment drops down to 50 degrees.

So what were these researchers witnessing? A free giveaway of heat and warmth, compassion at the level of a plant? Well, of course not. As sacred as this lotus is, it has a motive. Researchers speculate that this thermogenic "compassion" is intended as a kind of overnight motel for the insects that pollinate the flower.

own your motive, own your life force

Neti it out: *I am not a saint.*

It's time to neti out martyr identity. To do so, we need to examine the notion of choice. A choice is an act of conscious selection between two or more options. The option selected is the one preferred, and thus a choice is an expression of preference. Any choice is—even if you are choosing between two very bad options. This is what we mean when we say that we chose "the lesser of two evils." Choosing this way, as undesirable as it is in general, is nevertheless a preferred option. Thus, *any* choice is an action toward well-being. If granted, any choice is a satisfaction of a desire, even if that desire is for nothing more than a lesser evil. Whatever the choice may be, if you made it, you freely expressed a preference.

What's left is to own your motivation and to live with the consequences of your choice. Not to do so would be unfair to others. If, for example, you're putting in long days at work because you rely on stellar performance to feel good about yourself, it just wouldn't be fair to reproach your family by reminding them of how hard you work. Sure, they might benefit from the extra money you bring home, but,

let's face it, you aren't doing it for them—you're doing it for you.
Enjoy rather than reproach! If you are doing it for you, they owe
you nothing. Instead of reminding others of what they owe you, be
mindful of your own motives. Own your motives in order not to
be a martyr. To own your motives is to own your humanity. Dis-
identify from the ideal of saintly selflessness, from this notion that
you shouldn't have a motive. Accept your inevitable humanity. Yes,
you do have a motive—and there is nothing wrong with that. Your
motives make you human. Conclude: *I am not a saint.*

---

water the lotus seed:
neti doll meditation

Neti out the distinction between nothing and everything.

You've probably seen those wooden nesting dolls from Russia. They're
called *matryoshka*, and they come in varying sets. You open the outermost doll to find another one inside. You open that one, and there is
yet another doll inside. And so it goes until you get to the innermost
doll, which itself is indivisible.

Let's say that this nesting doll is a representation of you: each doll
is a layer of identification, with the innermost doll being your core
self, your essence. Now let's add a Sunyata twist to this. Let's put
the innermost doll aside for now and then neti the rest of the dolls
one layer of identification at a time. So, you remove the outer layer
of circumstance to find the layer of body. You then remove the body
layer, and you find the layer of the mind. As you remove this last,
innermost layer, that of the mind, what do you find? Nothing, right?
As you shed this last layer of information about you (your thoughts,
feelings, and sensations), you are left with empty hands, with nothing
in between. That's the Sunyata doctrine: it tells you that when you
strip away all the information that you call "you," you find nothing
solid.

But here's the glitch. Sure, you didn't find that indivisible, individual core doll of self that you presumed was there, but what you did find is hardly a nothing. Look at the expanse of the reality right in between your open hands; notice everything that immediately exists, everything you see, everything you feel, everything you smell and sense right now, the entire world! Hardly a nothing, huh? If this is a nothing, it's the kind of nothing that is full of everything.

Now let's put the innermost doll of individual, core self back into the doll set and try this again. Imagine yourself once again removing one layer of identifications at a time. You remove the outermost doll. After all, you are not your circumstance. Done! You open up the body-identification doll. After all, you are not your body. Done! Same with the mind doll: you are not your mind (thoughts, feelings, sensations, and so on). Done! So, now you are down to this indivisible, final, core-self doll. Seems like you found something uniquely you, something in particular. But have you?

So, here you sit, holding this small, indivisible doll of self with both of your hands. You're likely sitting on a chair that is stationed on the floor of the room you are in, which is structurally a part of some kind of domicile. This entire structure sits on a foundation, which, in its turn, rests on the ground, which is part of this planet. Earth is part of this solar system, which is part of the Milky Way galaxy, which is part of this infinite Universe. As you hold this innermost you, ponder this: is this really a separate self if it is fundamentally embedded and inescapably nested inside everything else? As you sit with this indivisible doll in your hand, you are holding a connection to everything else that exists. Having found an indivisible core doll of self inside you, you've also found a connection to everything else. This finding, by definition, negates the very notion of self as being separate.

Recognize that both of these scenarios (something inside, nothing inside) have *an identical happy ending*. What you find at the end of this neti-neti ego striptease is the kind of nothing that is everything. Recognize that *a nothing that is everything isn't a nothing*. Lotus identity identifies either with nothing or with everything—and there is no difference. Recall Zhuangzi and his thought about whether he was a man dreaming he was a butterfly or a butterfly dreaming it was a man. Are you a nothing dreaming you're everything, or are you everything dreaming you are a nothing? Is there a difference? Conclude: *If I am connected to everything, I am not a nothing.*

---

get real

Recognize that whatever you find when you strip yourself down to your informational negligee—nothing or everything—is not an illusion. The famous French philosopher Rene Descartes who, just like you, went in search of himself, concluded: "I think, therefore I am." I agree with the conclusion (that he was), but I find the necessity to evidence one's existence completely redundant. You *are*! Whether you are thinking or not, if you are, you are. What further evidence do you need of your self-existence? Am-ness is self-evident. Whether you want to call yourself "this," "that," "both this and that," or "neither this nor that," you are no illusion. If you are reading this, you know what I'm talking about. You bought this book, didn't you? You did. You are reading it right now, aren't you? You are. What illusion then? Get real!

conclusion: an illusion that exists is no illusion

Modern-day scientific empiricism and reductionism is a form of Western Sunyata. Western logicians reduce our sense of self to a marvelous illusion, a mirage of personal consistency that is a function of high-order neural-feedback loops. If we agree that we are nothing but a self-referencing daydream, then tell me this: who is the one who is dreaming? If we are, indeed, nothing but an illusion, then we are an illusion that exists. An illusion that exists, by definition, is not an illusion. If we are nothing but a mirage, then we are a mirage that exists. A mirage that exists, by definition, is not a mirage. If all we are is a ghost in the machine, then we are a ghost that exists. A ghost that exists, by definition, is not a ghost. If we are going to agree that perception is reality, then why should we, in the same breath, deny the reality of this perceptual reality? In conclusion, I invite you to water the seeds of your lotus identity one more time.

PART 3

re-identify with what you are

CHAPTER 5

the root of am-ness

Remember that your essence is experienced by you as a feeling. The trap is this: wanting to know who you are, which means you want to be able to say some words, think a thought, cling to a description. The question becomes: how can I find out what my essence is? There is nothing to find out. Remember it. Experience it. Feel the feeling of it. Let go of your thoughts, let the talk inside your head drift away, be still and remember who you are.

Paul Williams

Ask the question, "Who am I?" The question should be deeply rooted in you, like a new seed nestled deep in the soft earth and damp with water.

Thich Nhat Hanh

Consciousness is the essence of self (soul).

S. Radhakrishnan & C. A. Moore

Lotus identity is a habit of identification with self-as-consciousness (self-as-essence, self-as-spirit, self-as-soul) coupled with informational/identity detox. In this chapter, we practice how to re-identify with your essential self nonverbally, beyond descriptions, privately. In so doing, we continue to water the lotus seeds. We continue to take root in am-ness.

Consciousness Is Self-Consistent

There has never been a thought that didn't dissolve, that didn't go away, that didn't disappear, that wasn't replaced by another thought, by another object of consciousness (be it a feeling or an image or a memory). The fact is that the mind is inconsistent. Whenever you sample the mind, it's always different. Sure, it repeats and recycles certain thoughts like a holiday jingle. But that's hardly consistent enough.

Consciousness, on the other hand, is always the same. If you practice the various am-ness meditations I'll offer in this chapter, you'll discover that what's in the gap between the thoughts is always the same. Informational emptiness is uniform. Interpretive silence is always the same. Consciousness is self-consistent enough to be a foundation of self. Re-identify with what you always are, not with your transient mind forms and external identifications; with your true nature, not with the way that it has been nurtured; with your essence, not with the forms and patterns that it takes.

peel the informational onion

Many people meditate with their eyes closed or with their vision fixed on a set spot or item. These techniques facilitate concentration by creating a degree of sensory deprivation. Information distracts us from ourselves. Sensory deprivation reduces information and brings us closer to ourselves, helping us remove each layer of information that covers us.

Let's see what happens when you begin to peel the informational onion. First, go to a room without any external light source and turn off the light. Stand in the dark. Notice what happens. First you are still trying to see. But there's nothing to see. There is no visual input. Then you begin to listen. If it's quiet or if the room is relatively soundproof, the auditory layer falls away. If there is no tactile input (like a breeze) or olfactory input (fragrance), you begin to notice your thoughts. The mind replaces the external input with thoughts, images, and feelings. Fragments of conversations float up. Questions arise out of the blue. The mind streams. But after a while, the mind goes blank or, rather, drops out. The stream stops. In the increasing gaps between the thoughts, you finally see you. There you are, just standing. Nothing to it. Nothing special about it. Just you—pure presence. What was standing here before was a head full of mindlessly streaming mind. What's standing here now is a head full of empty presence, a head full of consciousness mindful of itself.

the field of growth

Find (or imagine) a field of grass or a spacious lawn. Sit down somewhere in the middle. Look around. Notice all the blades of grass quivering in the breeze. How many of them do you think are there? Tens of thousands? Maybe millions? Your consciousness is just as vast, just as plentiful. All these blades of grass, all these blossoming flowers, all these bending stems are like all the thoughts you've had, all the feelings you've felt, all the sensations you have experienced. Think about all the scents you've smelled in your life so far, all the things you have seen, all the thoughts you've had. Think about all the sensations you've experienced, all the things you have touched. Think of all the reality that you have experienced that became feelings, sensations, and thoughts. Think about all this visual, tactile, gustatory, and auditory information that has taken root in your consciousness in the form of impressions, memories, and reflexes. All of this is the contents of you. Memories of all the approvals you have earned and of all the approvals you have lost, ideas you've shared and ideas you've saved, all the resolved and unresolved issues, and, of course, plans, dreams, intentions, and ambitions yet to be completed or pursued. Somewhere in there might be a memory of your first kiss, the name of your first dog, the smell of the ocean, or a poem you wrote that you never shared with anyone. All of this is part of your growth.

But just as a sphere has an infinite number of sides but only one center, all this is a part of you, and no single part of this *is* you. Somehow, you—with this unmistakable sense of am-ness—are underneath it all. You are the ground, the soil, a plane of am-ness that is the basis of all this experience. What is there to judge about this sense of am-ness if it is the foundation of all judgment? Sit down, watch this field of self-growth, and recognize that you are the field, not just what grows on it or out of it. Sure, you could focus on a beautiful flower and think, "I am this." That would be self-esteem at the expense of the rest of what and who you are. Why focus on one flower and ignore the rest of the field? Sure, this good feeling would blossom; but only until the season changes, until the flower wilts, until somebody tramples upon it.

So spend some time in this field. Experience yourself as the entire space, not as the objects in it. And when you're done, leave; go, knowing that all of this overwhelming variety, all these blades of self-growth, all these thoughts, memories, sensations, and feelings aren't you. That's why you can get up and leave all this outside your awareness while still remaining yourself. Take no flowers with you. Carry no image.

am-ness, not I-ness, as a base of identity

Whenever you pause to watch your mind, it initially seems to flow without pause. Thoughts, sensations, feelings, and images succeed each other in a seemingly seamless procession. After a while, however, you begin to experience moments of pure awareness. At such moments, there are no forms to perceive. You are thoughtless, but mindfully so. Mindfully mindless. You are still aware, but of nothing in particular. Mindful with nothing on your mind. Aware, but not focused on anything. Seeing rather than looking. You just *are*. That's *am-ness*. That's *you*. In this space between the thoughts, in this gap between mind events, you glimpse your own consciousness. Or, to be exact, the consciousness glimpses itself.

Take the opportunity to glimpse this real you, the you that doesn't change. Practice recognizing the witness you, the observer you, the permanent you. Feel the reality of the uppercase Self, not the lowercase self, the you that is independent of success and failure. This you is naturally perfect—not because you are better than someone else or are accomplished at doing something—but because you are informationally unstained. This is the you that falls asleep at the end of the day after you have let go of the last pestering thought that stands in the way of your rest. This is the you that wakes up in the morning with nothing more than a sense of presence before your mind begins winding up with the stress and anxiety of daily striving. This is the you that you have always been, in between all your moments of glory and defeat. And this is the you that you will continue to remain until you are no longer. You might as well get to know this you. Learning to access this state of am-ness is the process of reengaging with your essential, immutable sense of self. This is *re-identification*.

am-track

Make an audio recording of the following series of questions. "What am I?" (Pause for thirty seconds.) "Who is this who is thinking right now?" (Pause for thirty seconds.) "Who is this who is wondering what she is?" (Pause for thirty seconds.) "Who is this who keeps referring to himself as 'I'?" (Pause for thirty seconds.) "Who is this who is thinking this thought right now?" (Pause for thirty seconds.) "Who is this who is sitting here and listening to this audio?" (Pause for thirty seconds.) "Who is this who keeps asking 'Who is this?'" (Pause for thirty seconds.) "Who is this who is recognizing that she isn't who she thinks she is?" (End the recording.)

Sit, close your eyes, and listen to your recording. Each and every time you hear one of these questions, say: "I am." Dis-identify from any other thoughts that pop into your mind. Override them with this simple truth: "Who is this?"; "I am." As you chant this simple answer, notice the one chanting. Board this Amtrack train of thought. Lay down the rails of am-ness to help yourself not get derailed by future identifications with the external.

the mind can be changed— consciousness can't

Whereas the path of dis-identification (the neti-neti path) establishes that you are not the mind stream (that you are not the ever-changing parade of thoughts, sensations, feelings, and memories), the re-identification path allows you to sink the anchor of your identity into the permanence of consciousness. The mind can be changed. Consciousness can't. Others can change your mind about your mind (that is, your thoughts about yourself, your feelings about yourself). But others cannot change your consciousness (as long as you stay out of boxing rings and don't hang out in front of a shotgun). That's what makes consciousness sturdy ground on which your identity can stand.

the chicken-or-the-egg of a breath, part 1

Close your eyes and notice your breathing. Leave it as it is—there is no need to manipulate it. Depending on where you begin, you first notice yourself either taking in a breath or exhaling it. Pay attention to this for a while. Recognize that after you inhale, you exhale. And after you exhale, you inhale. Now open your eyes and ponder for a minute: which comes first? Do you inhale first, or do you exhale first? Close your eyes and attend to your breath. As you keep watching the breath, keep wondering what comes first. Read no further. Watch the breath and ponder this. When ready, come back to part 2.

the chicken-or-the-egg of a breath, part 2

Close your eyes again and notice your breathing. Notice the inhalation, notice the exhalation (in whichever sequence you notice first). Now, see that after you inhale, there is a brief pause. When you're breathing fast, the pause is pretty much imperceptible. But when you are breathing calmly, the pause is there.

Notice this pause: you are no longer inhaling, and you are not yet exhaling. Now, notice the pause after you exhale. If you are breathing calmly, the pause is long enough to register. Notice this space: you are no longer exhaling, and you are not yet inhaling. Recognize that it's the same pause.

Now, let's go back to the chicken-or-the-egg question. What comes first in a breath cycle: an inhalation or exhalation? Not at birth, but in the present. What comes first (at least when you're breathing slowly) is this space of nothingness, this moment of emptiness. It's both the beginning of the breath cycle and the end of it. When you are paying attention to your breath, you are of the mind. You are consumed by the sensation of the breath. But when you are in between the breaths, there is no breath to distract you from you-as-consciousness. As the breath dissolves, you find nothing. Not the kind of nothing that doesn't exist, not absolute absence, but the kind of nothing that has nothing to describe. This is the kind of nothing that exists but has no qualities, the nothing of pure awareness, the nothing of witnessing, the nothing of consciousness on standby. And this moment of nothingness provides you with a glimpse of information-free am-ness, of the consciousness behind the mind, a fleeting vision of the original you. This is, admittedly, a glimpse of nothing special. And that's what makes it a glimpse of permanence.

---

am-ness as a point of view

Consciousness is awareness. Awareness is always *of* something. We aren't just aware, *we are aware of.* Awareness is a point of view, a localized perspective of looking out. This "reference point, the 'I,'" says U. G. Krishnamurti, "cannot be eliminated through any volition on your part" (2002b, 156). This "reference point," this point of view, *is* you. Thus, awareness inadvertently divides us into a witness and that which we are witnessing.

Being aware is the same as being a self, a witness. For all intents and purposes, being aware of being aware is self-awareness. Thus, purposeful awareness manipulation is an intuitive and simple way of reconnecting with your in-dwelling self. We can rewrite this idea schematically as follows:

1. Being aware = being oneself

2. Being aware of being aware (which is the same as 1) = self-awareness

3. Self-awareness = awareness of self as being separate

The following three exercises are most useful when done one after the other. This first exercise will help you utilize awareness-manipulation strategies as a way of re-identifying with your sense of self. Here's your chance to learn how to shift your point of view on demand.

drive your attention

As you sit, begin to visually scan the environment around you, stopping at each object of your attention for just long enough to have the feeling of "I am now looking at such and such." Instead of our usual, seamless visual participation, be a bit robot-like, grotesquely purposive and deliberate. As you move your head around, let it literally come to a halt as you decide on a point of view. Notice how each and every time you decide to fix your attention on this or that, there's an instant amplification of your sense of self. The very act of choosing a point of view dials up the sense of am-ness.

Keep deploying your attention deliberately like this to keep catching a glimpse of yourself. Notice that this feeling of am-ness evaporates rather quickly. As you move your head, let's say you decide to pause on the electrical outlet in the wall. As soon as you do, you notice yourself. And as soon as you notice yourself, your mind rushes to obscure this sense of presence. The following analogy might bring this into focus for you. Say that you're riding in a car, in the passenger's seat. You're mindlessly enjoying the scenery when the driver suddenly taps the brakes. As your body moves forward and presses against the restraining seatbelt, you suddenly notice yourself; but as the driver eases up on the brakes and resumes the usual speed, you once again become a passive, mindless passenger, and your sense of self-awareness fades out.

There appears to be something rather similar going on when we stop our head movement during our visual scan. It's as though the mind that was just riding along suddenly bumps into that innermost self that had made the conscious choice to stop its mindless ride. So, keep scanning and stopping. Keep consciously deploying your attention to catch a glimpse of that innermost self.

stop and go

As a follow-up to the previous exercise, try to deliberately lift up a cup from the surface of the table. Notice how the original fluid mindlessness of the movement is gone and now you are in this jerky stop-and-go mode of making micro-decisions and then executing them. Notice that you fade in and out as you stop and go. As you stop, you fade in. As you go, you fade out. We seem to lose ourselves in action and find ourselves in choice.

rest in self-view

Now as another awareness-manipulation experiment, let's add an element of purposeful self-awareness. Focus your point of view on yourself as you drive your attention around. As you turn your head and deliberately shift your point of view, maintain an awareness of yourself doing this. In your mind, run the following narrative: "Here, I am choosing to pause to look at this... Here, I am choosing to resume my attention to the target search... Here I am choosing to pause and look at that... Here I am continuing to look at that..." In other words, allow yourself to consciously rest in your point of view while at the same time casting a quick glance at the viewer. When you find something visually appealing to focus on, pause and notice this ping-pong of attention: first you are looking out, then you are looking at the one who is looking. Notice that the first looking is visual, and the second kind of looking is more like knowing. Notice this difference.

Let me offer you an image that can help you conceptualize what is going on. Let's say that you have a third eye right in the middle of your forehead. In Indian thought, the third eye is "the eye of the inward look" (Organ 1970, 65). So, here you sit, looking at, say, a tree through the window. As you look at the tree, your two regular eyes are wide open, but the third eye (let's call it the "mind's eye") is half closed. As you decide to notice yourself looking, as you choose to become aware of being aware, your two regular eyes kind of glaze over and the mind's eye, the one in the middle of your head, opens up wide. Using this picture as a map of this experience, practice resting in this two-way view, noticing this out-looking/in-looking ping-pong of attention. Notice the world, notice you, notice the world, notice you.

the truth of am-ness

The point of this book is to help you dis-identify from your false self and learn to re-identify with your true self. The process of dis-identification is a process of disillusionment. Usually, we think of the word "disillusionment" as something negative, but as soon as we inject a hyphen into this word "dis-illusionment" becomes something positive. After all, the only way to see the reality of what you are is to shed the illusions of what you are. Dis-illusionment is awakening from a dream in which you were dreaming that you are this or that to realize that you are neither this nor that.

awakening to am-ness

Set an alarm for five minutes and then lie down. Close your eyes as if you were sleeping, and start thinking about yourself the way you usually do. Think, "I am such and such... I am like this or like that..." Simulate your informational identity. Think like ego does. "I am good, bad, so and so, such and such..." Remind yourself of your roles and identities: "I am such and such..." Then, as soon as you hear the alarm, open your eyes to wake up from the dream of this false self and immediately get up (not so fast that you faint!). Recognize that you are not the informational dream that you just had. Realize: *I am that which is awake and aware now.* Repeat this a few times to learn to access the truth of am-ness.

am-ness as mindfulness

Vipassana-style mindfulness is an excellent access point to am-ness because it allows you to be the witness. When you climb up on that bank of the river to watch your mind flow, you become the subject, the observer of whatever is passing near you or through you. You, the subject, begin to observe your own mind objects. Each and every time you dis-identify from a mind object passing through you, you inadvertently re-identify with yourself as a subject. Each and every time you passively notice an object of consciousness (a thought, a feeling, a sensation, or an image) pass through your field of awareness, you are staying attuned to what remains—the essential you. This distillation of experience into the subject and the object that is integral to vipassana-style mindfulness is the very heart of self-cleaning. Review the mindfulness exercises that I introduced in chapter 4 and consider developing a mindfulness practice as a doorway to yourself and an all-around identity detox program.

I am what I am and other pointers

Re-identification doesn't have to be experiential. It can be verbal, with the help of what Lama Surya Das, a Dzogchen lama, calls "pithy instructions." A pithy instruction is a powerful catchphrase that pivots your mind toward what matters—in this case, away from itself (2005, 22). Take the tautological phrase "I am what I am," made famous by Popeye. This simple phrase can powerfully and promptly anchor your sense of identity in yourself, rescuing your essence out of the jungle of arbitrary evaluations. Ken Wilber's phrase "I am what remains" (after you have dis-identified from everything you are not) is another powerful verbal anchor for essence. The Hindu greeting "Namaste," if understood in the sense of "the essence/consciousness in me acknowledges the essence/consciousness in you," can also serve as a kind of verbal bow to self. Or you may use the Upanishadic dis-identification mantra *neti-neti* in combination with a verbal re-identification, as follows: "Not this, not that! I am what I am!" Of course, none of this verbal self-reference has the magic touch to turn form into essence, but these kinds of verbal formulas quickly and effectively point your attention toward you.

the space of am-ness

One of my favorite definitions of what we are comes from Dzogchen/Tibetan Buddhism. Dzogchen's term for consciousness is *rigpa*, which has been defined as "space that is aware." Indeed, stripped down to our essence, we seem to be nothing more than a field of awareness, a space with a point of view. Not an emptiness, in the sense of a vacuum, but a kind of zone of presence that, on one hand, is aware of itself and, on the other hand, is ever ready, like the surface of a mirror, to reflect any information passing by.

Self: 3-D or 2-D?

I prefer the metaphor of a field of awareness to that of the surface of a mirror, because experientially, this sense of self-presence feels 3-D, not 2-D. But here's a curious thing. Whether this sense of self feels 3-D or 2-D (like a space or a reflective area) seems to depend on whether we have our eyes open or shut. This might not be true, but what I've observed in my own meditation practice is that looking out onto the world shallows out my sense of presence, deprives it of depth and vastness.

Test the parameters of your self-space. Sit in silence, intermittently opening and closing your eyes. Keep track of the "volume" of your self-space. Check to see if, by opening your eyes, your essence shallows out, becomes subsumed by your senses. Check to see if by closing your eyes you can expand your sense of self. See if the event horizon of your awareness shrinks or inflates in diameter depending on whether your eyes are "on" or not. Experiment to see what your am-ness feels like. Is it two-dimensional, mirror-like, surface deep, and all reflective, or is it three-dimensional, space-like, all embracing?

the dots and spaces

Remember the "dots" exercise in which you watched "the river of consciousness" and each and every time you recognized a thought you marked a dot ("watching the river")? If not, please go back to chapter 3 and review this exercise before you proceed.

Now, let's try it again, but this time we'll be working with an element of breath focus. You'll need a pen or pencil, a piece of paper—and your lungs. Begin by paying attention to your breath. Simply notice your breath as it is. As soon as you are distracted by a thought or some other sensation, put down a dot on the piece of paper. As soon as you put down a dot, return to the awareness of your breath. Keep at this for a few minutes. Go ahead and do this first step or you will spoil the effect of the conclusions, ruining the punch line. So, put the book down now and mark your dots.

Okay, now that you're done with the first part of the exercise, take a good look at your piece of paper. Recognize that the dots correspond to mental events, to mind events. Each dot was some kind of thought, some kind of informational event, an object of consciousness, a slice of the mind stream. Now, what about the spaces in between the dots? What do you think the spaces could stand for? These fleeting moments of emptiness, these spaces between the thoughts, these moments of pure awareness, these moments of informationally untainted am-ness, that is...you. You are not the mind dots. They are a part of you but no more than a reflection is a part of the mirror. You are the space in between these mind dots. Now, try this exercise again. Settle into the *space* that you are. Take a note of this sense of unqualified and indescribable presence: here you are, the real you, the one that doesn't change, simply here, not going anywhere, invulnerable and unafraid. It's nothing special! And that's what makes it permanent.

location, location, location

Am-ness is not a thought; it is not an informational layer. Am-ness is a direct experience of self, not an indirect self-reference. Am-ness is self-knowledge, not self-description. Here's what I mean. Go to your bathroom mirror. While there, ponder this. You've been in front of this mirror with a different face every time you looked into it. As far as this mirror is concerned, it has never seen the same face twice. But how often have you wondered if this is still the same mirror? Probably never. You *know* that this is the same mirror. But how? Read no further (if you are planning to do this exercise, go ahead and do it, giving yourself a chance to ponder it first before you let me ponder it for you). Make sure you go to the mirror now and actually do this thinking. Bring the book with you.

Now, after you've pondered your relationship with your bathroom mirror, look into it again. Consider: if you were to step aside and let somebody else reflect in this mirror, you'd still *know* it is the same mirror, even though the reflection displayed on the mirror would be entirely different. But how would you know this? You'd know it's the same mirror because it's in the same place. The answer is so obvious that it might have not immediately occurred to you. That's how it is with things we know. We don't really think about them. We just know.

Your point of view is a permanent location. That's why you know exactly where it is. It's right here, wherever you are right now. You are always here. This "here" is the location of your am-ness. It never changes. You are never anywhere else but here. Whether you're in a chair reading this exercise or in the bathroom with this book in hand, you are in your own space of consciousness. You bring this space with you. Like an ingenious traveler, you bring with you your own here, your own destination to wherever you go. Wherever you are aware, you are aware *here*, not somewhere there, outside of you. And it's exactly because you are always here, wherever your point of view is, that you know yourself from what you are not. In other words, you are a space that is aware of its own location. You are a location of your awareness wherever—geographically—that might be. Wherever your am-ness is, there you are. If you know where you are, you know you.

So, whenever you find yourself informationally lost, ask yourself: where am I? As soon as you pose this question, you know the answer and you know you. "Where am I?" is a question that simultaneously satisfies our two criteria for essence: locality and permanence. The locality of your point of view *is* your permanence! "Where am I growing now?" Right here. "Where am I searching for myself?" Right here. "Where am I alive right now?" Right here. "Where am I?" Right here. "I am where I am" is the same as "I am what I am." Know your location and know you. Realizing that you are here and now isn't a thought, it's *self-evident knowledge*; it's not thinking, it's self-seeing.

a caveat on the permanence of consciousness

Early in the book, I claimed that everything is impermanent. Now, here we have the idea that am-ness is ever present. If everything is impermanent, if everything is changing, then how can I assert that consciousness is a permanent-enough basis for identity? Let me clarify this point.

Objectively, nothing is permanent. Subjectivity—the mirror of your consciousness, your sense of am-ness—is permanent while you are alive. From a purely psychological (not spiritual) point of view, while you are alive, you are always alive. You will be alive until the very last moment of your life. Your consciousness will not experience its own death, because your-mind-the-journalist, your-mind-the-narrator will not be there to report on the disappearance of the very consciousness it's made of. After all, it is only through the narrative of the mind that we learn about what happens to us. As the famous logician Ludwig Wittgenstein proclaims in his *Tractatus Logico-Philosophicus*, first published in 1922: "Death is not an event in life: we do not live to experience death" (2007, 87).

So, it is in this sense that I propose that your consciousness is permanent. Whether consciousness continues after your body dies is a matter of religious, scientific, and metaphysical speculation that is outside of the scope of this book. In sum, we are talking not about the immortality of your consciousness, but about its subjective permanence.

water the lotus seed: the bowl is already broken

This isn't an am-ness access meditation but an experiential illustration of the point above. Grab any bowl from your cupboard. Fill it up with hot water, then pour the water out. Fill it up with cold water, then pour it out. Put some soapy water in the bowl. Pour it out. Wad up a paper towel and stuff it into the bowl. Shake it out of the bowl. Put your keys in the bowl. Take them out.

Thanks for your patience. Here's my point: you are just like this bowl. Your consciousness is a container of information. Each moment, the bowl of your consciousness fills up with this mind or that mind. While the bowl lasts, its holding capacity is a constant. But, of course, the bowl itself isn't permanent. In the bigger picture of time, the bowl's already broken. The actual "when" is just a matter of time. This is another great reason to avoid holding on to your fleeting informational contents. Now and then, wash the bowl of its preoccupations. Set it aside, and let its informational residue dry out. Rest in your informational emptiness. Be a bowl while you are one.

---

am-ness as psychological "re-incarnation"

Whereas consciousness dies once (assuming there is no afterlife), mind dies all the time. Mind—the stream of thoughts, feelings, memories, images, and perceptions—is constantly dissolving, constantly dying (psychologically speaking).

Let's say you had a perfect driving record, and you thought of yourself as a perfect driver. Then you get a speeding ticket, and your previous self-concept (a mind object) dies. Or, you were an A student, but after you got your first B, you felt that something died, that something ended. Indeed, something has perished: an identification died. And so we keep grieving the death of our mind forms from one identity crisis to another, from one ego crisis to another. The mind dies a billion thought deaths. Re-identification with your real self, with your sense of am-ness, is a kind of re-incarnation, a kind of psychological rebirth.

---

real-time you

Try the following meditational approach as a kind of experiential re-incarnation of your essence. Aim to be a real-time you. Eat when you eat. Walk when you walk. Practice being one moment at a time, one step at a time, one breath a time. For how long? For however long you feel you need to feel reborn in your essence. For however long it takes for you to re-identify with the one who is living.

false self out, real self in

Ilchi Lee, a Korean meditation teacher, says that "life begins with exhalation" and "by emptying oneself" (2005, 41). Building on this thought, try this imagery: as you inhale, take in a real self, and as you exhale, let out your false self. In—essence; out—form. In—truth; out—falsehood. In—what is; out—what isn't. In—real self; out—false self.

lotus breath 1

Sit down with your eyes closed. Let your chin hang over your chest. Sit like this for a few moments. Imagine yourself as a lotus flower closed off for the night: your head a bundle of beautiful petals, resting on the stem of your neck; your leaf shoulders spread atop the placid surface of a pond. Now inhale. As you breathe in, lift up your chin gracefully, as though you were a swan, while simultaneously opening your eyes. Inhale the sky of what is, the reality of what is immediately given. Allow yourself to take it all in—all that you see, all that you hear, all that you smell. And without stopping, in one graceful, flowing motion, begin to exhale your way down to your original resting position as you close your eyes.

As you exhale what is, notice you, the one who is breathing. With your chin down, pause comfortably before the next breath, catching another glimpse of the you that resides between what is and what isn't. Breathe in. Breathe out. And once again, blossom out into the sky of what is, lifting your chin, opening your eyes, taking it all in. And just as soon as your in-breath reaches its apex, begin to let go of everything your consciousness just touched by exhaling all that no longer is. Repeat generously. Self-cleanse with lotus breath until you feel more informationally pure.

lotus breath 2

In the book *The Blooming of a Lotus: Guided Meditations for Achieving the Miracle of Mindfulness,* author Thich Nhat Hanh offers this: "Breathing in, I see myself as a flower. Breathing out, I feel fresh." He adds: "We breathe in to restore the flower in us. This in-breath brings the flower in us back to life. The out-breath helps us be aware that we have the capacity to be, and are now, fresh as a flower. This awareness waters our flower; this is the practice of loving-kindness meditation toward ourselves" (1999, 23–24). Take Thich Nhat Hanh's advice: eyes closed or open, sit in self-purification. Breathing in, see yourself as a lotus flower; breathing out, feel yourself cleansed.

conclusion: self-remembering

As I noted above, re-identification with your essential self is a habit of self-remembering. George Gurdjieff, a Greek-Armenian "rascal sage" who grew up in pre-Soviet Russia, emphasized the importance of incorporating meditation into real life. One of his exercises was essentially an attempt to condition oneself to connect self-remembering/re-identification with something as trivial and commonplace as walking through a door. So, as we close this chapter, let me offer you the following suggestion. Consider getting into a habit of thinking of each doorway as a threshold of essence. As you walk in and out of various rooms in your life, consider associating the very passage through a doorway as a kind of self-re-entry. So, whether you are walking out of your home or stepping into your office, whether you are boarding a bus or departing a train, see the openings as space allowing you to recognize your essence. And, if you happen to be carrying any luggage of identification, consider leaving this informational burden at the door. *Exhale what isn't* to leave what you are not behind. *Inhale what still is* to notice who is passing through.

PART 4

perennial growth

CHAPTER 6

lotus blossom

One's real person (self) [is] same as the world-ground…This, verily, is that!

Upanishads

The Soul [insert any other term for real self here, consciousness, essence, spirit, and so on] is not composed of any materials. It is unity indivisible. Therefore it must be indestructible. For the same reasons it must also be without any beginning. So the Soul is without beginning and end.

Vivekananda

Everything is your original self that is perfectly without lack and is completely fulfilled in itself. Don't be surprised… It's in the Lotus Sutra, isn't it!

Hakuun Yasutani

What you call the spirit of the times is fundamentally the… mind, in which the times are reflected.

Faust, in Johann Wolfgang von Goethe's *Faust*

Lotus identity is identification with consciousness, not mind. As such, lotus identity is a potential promotion of individual identity to a level of global or even cosmic identity. You don't have to promote your individual identity to that level, but you can.

identifying with the bigger picture

Take a look at the following thought: "When you start to see that you are ever changing and cannot be fixed in time and space, and that the nature of the entire world is ever changing and cannot be fixed in time and space, you might ask the question: Then where did I go? You didn't go anywhere. The idea of self is an illusion. As you practice Zen, you will start to see that... the separation of you and the cow and the river and the world is all an illusion" (Sach and Faust 2004, 138).

What does this mean? It means that, as your fixed self disappears, as you drop the illusion of being separate, you become everything (the cow you are watching on the other side of the river, the river itself, and the world at large). Sunyata doctrine of no self does not get rid of the essential self—it merely lets it out of the informational cage of the ego to join with the rest of the world. So, as the false self is laid off, the essential self gets a promotion. In the process of dis-identifying from all this that you used to call you, the real you becomes all that.

---

what's in a name?

Lotus blossom: *I am that which is nameless.*

Imagine a thousand people of different nationalities pointing at the moon from a thousand different places. Recognize that everybody's pointing at the same object but a) from different vantage points/locations and b) in different ways (with different hands, different fingers).

Now, imagine that you could ask all of these people to name what they are seeing. You'd hear a thousand different names. Recognize that, despite all of these differences (in perspective and description), the moon is still the same. In fact, the moon is nameless.

Recall from our previous look into the mirror of language that we established that no description or name equals that which it describes or names. Innumerable famed and obscure logicians, theologians, scientists, saints, philosophers, monks, priests, shamans, poets, writers, and common folk gazed at this sky within us and the sky outside of us, and they all saw some kind of organizing principle, some kind of unifying basis of identity. Some called it matter, others called it consciousness, and yet others called it spirit, buddha nature, Brahman, Dao, and so on and so forth. But the moon of that insight remains as nameless as it ever was. What's in a name? Nothing but a description of that which is nameless. Ponder this. Conclude: *I am that which is nameless. I am that which cannot be named.*

---

one-is-all/all-is-one: a path of compassion

Upanishads, a set of ancient Hindu scriptures, speaks of the equality of individual consciousness (*atman*) and cosmic consciousness (*Brahman*). This idea is captured in the phrase *"aham Brahmasmi,"* which translates as "I (atman, individual self) am Brahman (cosmic, universal, global self)" or as "the core of my being is the ultimate reality, the root and ground of the universe, the source of all that exists" (Chopra 2003, 174). What an amazingly expansive and self-transcendent identification! Indeed, if I am all, then there is no difference between me and everything else. If I am all, then there is no separation between me and not-me. Whereas we used the neti-neti process (another Upanishadic idea) as a way of dis-identifying from what we are not, the *"aham Brahmasmi"* idea takes us toward a seemingly paradoxical conclusion: *you are that.*

In pondering similar issues, author Jerry Katz wrote: "When we seriously consider this non-separate reality, our identity becomes muddled. The walls that define who we are become flimsy and disappear. All things are seen as they are, without blockage or gauziness of walls. Things standing out shining" (2007, 190). Beautifully stated, isn't it? I agree with every one of these words except for one. Jerry Katz says that this all-is-one/one-is-all perspective makes our identity "muddled." I disagree: I think this perspective makes our identity finally pure, lotus-like, finally detoxed of all the informational mud that keeps us separate and existentially disenfranchised.

This Upanishadic idea that one-is-all/all-is-one is a powerful foundation for compassion. Indeed, if you believe that you aren't just you but everything—this, that, and the other—then you have no choice but to include in the sphere of your self-interest all that exists. You can see how this kind of global/cosmic/universal identification brings forth such ancient teachings as the doctrine of *ahimsa* or nonviolence. Traditions of pacifism, vegetarianism, veganism, and eco-mindedness take root in this kind of identification as well.

one on one with each other's consciousness

As soon as we allow for the possibility of relating to others on the basis of am-ness rather than I-ness, we run into a couple of provocative paradigm shifts.

One Essence

The first of these shifts is that, if you see yourself as consciousness, not mind—as essence and not form or information—and if you see others in the same way, then you begin to realize that, at the essential level, we are the same. We are different only in terms of information—in terms of thoughts, feelings, and sensations that pass through us, in terms of our informational contents, in the ways our essence has been shaped and programmed by the specific context we grew up in. But, of course, we aren't our informational contents or our informational context. Here's an exercise to help you appreciate this point.

zero difference

Lotus blossom: *In essence, I am that.*

Here's a simple experience to drive the point home. Get two differently shaped glasses or tumblers or cups out of your cupboard. Put them side by side. Look at them. In form they are different. One's tall, the other's short. Or, one has a handle, the other doesn't. Perhaps they are of different sizes. But what's the same? Right now, they are equally empty. Emptiness is uniform. Emptiness is sameness. You and I are just like that. If we look at ourselves as consciousness, as pure awareness, as nothing but awareness of awareness, then there is no informational difference between us. Ponder this.

Next, fill the two containers with different contents. Look at them. Now, in addition to the external differences in form, these two containers are also filled with different contents. Once again, this is just like us. You and I have different bodily forms, and at any given point we are filled with different mind forms. But recall that if we identify ourselves as consciousness, not as minds, then these external and internal differences don't really matter. If we both subscribe to lotus-style identity, if we dis-identify from all this information, then there is seemingly zero informational difference between us.

You can try a similar experiment with two mirrors. Look at two mirrors. Notice the difference in reflections. Notice the similarity at the level of the mirrors themselves. Recognize that at our core, when stripped down of all our information, in our essence, we are all fundamentally the same. The only differences between us are context, body, and mind; the only differences between us are...our differences. But we are not our differences; we are not our shapes, forms, or information. All that is ever changing, passing, fleeting, and circumstantial. Conclude: *In essence, I am that.*

Identification-Based Forgiveness

The second paradigm-shifting implication of relating to each other on the basis of am-ness (consciousness) is this: identification leads to forgiveness. Indeed, when we can relate to what another person has done, when we can identify with their course of action, when we can see ourselves in their choices, reactions, and motives, we put ourselves firmly upon the path of forgiveness. Here's an exercise to help drive this point home.

to forgive, relate

Lotus blossom: *I forgive you your form
and I identify with your essence.*

Here's an identification-based forgiveness protocol for you to try.

1. Access a state of am-ness (via a method of your choice).

2. Recognize there is no essential difference between you and the offender, just informational difference

3. *Break* the state of am-ness with the thought: "I am you/him/her/them.

What you are doing here is first accessing your innermost sense of self (emptying the cup) and then identifying with the other person (filling your cup with a thought of identification with the offender). Try this out, privately, by forgiving those who you feel have harmed you in the past. Work through a couple of grudges using this method. Each and every time you apply this to a particular individual, recognize that you are forgiving their form (their words and/or actions) exactly because you are identifying with their essence. Note that just because you *can* forgive, it doesn't mean that you have to. This exercise offers you a formula for identification-based forgiveness. I do not mean to suggest that you absolutely should forgive. Forgiveness isn't an obligation. Forgiveness is a choice. The point of this exercise is to showcase one possible use of your blossoming lotus identity.

consciousness is a secret we all share

The word "consciousness" betrays the secret we all share. According to the Online Etymology Dictionary (www.etymonline.com), the word "consciousness" derives from the Latin word *conscius,* which—in its original, literal meaning—translates as "shared or common knowledge" (from the prefix *con,* which means "with," and the verb *scire,* which means "to know"). If you recall from our earlier discussion of the word "self," both the word "self" and the word "secret" stem from the Proto-Indo-European word stem *se,* meaning "separate."

Earlier in the book, I proposed that the self is a kind of secret that you cannot share. More specifically, I suggested that this secret has to do with your ability to tell you from not-you, to tell your essential sense of am-ness from all the passing information that it is not. We have since equated am-ness with consciousness. So, what we seem to have is a rather intriguing puzzle of identity. We all have this secret of being able to tell our consciousness/am-ness from what it is not. In essence, we know that at our core we are just that—am-ness, consciousness. We can also infer that others, at their core, are also nothing but this am-ness, nothing but this consciousness. Just as we now realize we aren't our circumstances, body, or mind, we can safely extrapolate that others are similarly not their circumstances, their bodies, or their minds.

It seems almost inexpressible, but it seems a safe guess that others, when also stripped of their information, are nothing but am-ness, their am-ness, their consciousness. So, by knowing ourselves, we know others. By knowing ourselves as consciousness, we can now recognize others as consciousness as well. *This = that. I am that. The consciousness in me recognizes the consciousness in you.* And, what if it is this very knowledge that was originally meant by the word "consciousness" itself? Consciousness, perhaps, *is* the shared knowledge that we all share, the same pivot of am-ness, the same consciousness, *the same unifying lotus secret of being not this, not that.*

If you were looking to anchor your restless mind to one word of all-pervading identity, the word "consciousness" would be a good reminder of the existential ground of being on which we all stand. But, of course, you can frame your lotus identity any way you want, perhaps through such words as "soul," "essence," "consciousness," "spirit," or "am-ness." Ultimately, it's not about what we call ourselves, but about what we know ourselves to be in our essence.

individual = universal

If you are interested in adding more cosmic petals to the lotus of your identity, to expand the radius of your identification, let us, in closing, consider the meaning of the word "individual" itself. Derived from the Latin prefix *in,* which means "not," and *dividuus,* which means "divisible" (by way of the Latin verb *divider,* "to divide"), the word "individual" literally means "indivisible" (www.etymonline.com). Ponder this.

1. **Indivisible = indestructible = foundational = essential.** If you are indivisible, then at your core, *you are the core of what*

is. If we cannot break something down, then we have reached the most essential dimension of what exists. If you are the indivisible, then you are (made of) that very basic layer of what exists, of the very essence that is the essence of everything else.

2. **Indivisible = indestructible = foundational = essential = inseparable.** If your essence is indivisible, then it is of the same stuff that is the foundation of all reality (foundational). If so, then you cannot be separated from the rest of what exists.

3. **Indivisible = indestructible = foundational = essential = inseparable = universal.** If you cannot be separated from the rest of what exists, then how can you be a *se*-lf, a *se*-parate entity? If, in your essence, you share in the essence of everything that exists, then your identity is the same as that of the rest of what exists—and individual becomes universal.

So, the seemingly separatist word "individual" means anything but separateness. It means one-with-all. Individual—if truly indivisible—equals universal.

conclusion: perennial identity

There are perennial flowers. There are also perennial ideas. The idea that, in your essence, you share in the essence of everything else that exists is a perennial idea. Upanishadic philosophers equated individual consciousness with all-pervading consciousness thousands of years ago. If consciousness is, indeed, everywhere, then there is no separating from it. Buddhist philosophers did the same a little later with the idea of buddha nature. Christians followed suit with the idea of spirit. Materialists throughout the ages conveyed the same idea of the all-pervading substance that underlies everything and called it matter.

Modern-day cosmologists speak of the same interrelatedness on the level of elemental particles.

It's all the same idea of fundamental interconnectedness stated through different terms and analyzed from different angles. Same moon—different hands, different fingers pointing at the indescribable unifying principle. This idea of essential interconnectedness, this idea that the essence of an individual is indivisible and is thus one with all, is an idea we can all relate to—a shared identity platform. But as beautiful an idea as it is, any idea is still a mind form, an informational weed. And this informational weed is called "lotus identity." No need to neti this one. Cultivate it instead. And now that this perennial seed of lotus identity is in you, too, take the opportunity to water it every chance you get. How? Turn the page.

CHAPTER 7

Identity-Detox Emergency Room

A single meditation can change people because it has allowed them to release part of the false self for good.

Deepak Chopra

Mother, father, child, wife, body, wealth—everything I can lose except my Self... bliss in the Self... This is individuality that never changes, and this is perfect.

Vivekananda

Who are you? You are who burns. You are who people see. You are who people never see. You are who lives at this address, this particular corner of space and time, moving through space and time, yet always your corner, your place, your space inside the circle of light—location of beingness— you. You are you. That doesn't sound like much, does it? But to the child who comes to you for comfort, it's more than enough. And all your wishes and coulds and didn'ts and shoulds don't matter. He is drawn to your I am.

Paul Williams

I want to leave you with a step-by-step process for "refinding yourself," to borrow a phrase from Carl Jung (2009, 231). Consider this chapter as a kind of identity-detox emergency room, as a starting point for restoring your sense of essential self when need be.

informational triage

Whenever you find yourself ruminating, obsessing, or dwelling on something you did or didn't do, or about something somebody said or possibly thought about you, or about how such-and-such reflects on who or what you are, you've got a case of *informational poisoning.* Time to pop into the identity-detox ER! Emergency informational detox starts out with an *informational triage*: the first order of self-help business is to figure out which mirror of identity you got trapped in.

Are You Stuck in the Physical Mirror?

Are you worried about your appearance, your looks, a new zit, a new wrinkle? Are you disgusted with your receding and/or gray hair? Are you having a bad hair day? Are you embarrassed about not having anything new to wear or feeling over- or underdressed? Have you confused you with your reflection in the physical mirror?

Are You Stuck in the Social Mirror?

Are you caught up in what so-and-so might have thought of you or said to you? Are you worried about others' opinion of you? Are you feeling dissed, invalidated, devalued, criticized, put down, unfairly judged, and misunderstood? Are you feeling wounded after receiving feedback? Are you jonesing for approval and compliments? Have you confused yourself with others' thoughts about you?

Are You Stuck in the Situational Mirror?

Are you dissatisfied with your station in life, with your social and economic circumstance? Are you worried about your reputation, your rank, your status, your popularity rating? Have you confused yourself with your circumstances and your situation?

Are You Stuck in the Relational Mirror?

Have you lost sight of who and/or what you are behind all your roles, duties, and obligations? Are you feeling that your essence has been eclipsed by your affiliations and relationships? Have you forgotten who and/or what you were before you became whoever you have relationally become (romantic partner, spouse, parent)? Have you over-identified with your football team (and it lost) or with a political party (and it lost)? Have you confused yourself with your relationships?

Are You Stuck in the Behavioral Mirror?

Are you preoccupied with something you did or didn't do? Are you in that "shoulda-coulda-woulda" vortex of rumination? Are you struggling to leave work at work? Are you worried about your professional identity and losing sleep over some performance outcome of yours? Are you beating yourself up for a grade you got or didn't get? Or have you over-identified with some pastime, hobby, or avocation to the point of having lost your sense of self? Are you over-identified with your meditation/spiritual practice, chasing enlightenment and starting to call yourself a Buddhist or some other label? Have you, in other words, confused yourself with what you do?

Are You Stuck in the Material Mirror?

Are you caught up in what you have or don't have says about you? Have you banged up your car and feel you can't get over it? Are you having house envy or iPhone envy? Are you constantly checking your stocks, fantasizing about what you'd do if you won the lottery, or working yourself to death to keep up with the Joneses? Are you stuck in some bitter financial or property dispute? Are you shopping yourself into debt? Have you, in other words, confused yourself with what you have or don't have?

Are You Stuck in the Bio-Data Mirror?

Are you hung up on your age or weight? Are you feeling "too old"? Are you hiding in a closet of some kind and worried what such and such physical preference of yours would say about you? Have you taken wellness to a level of obsession, spending all your discretionary income and time on trying to stay young? Have you, in effect, confused your sense of self with your body?

Are You Stuck in the Mirror of Time?

Has something happened and you feel you cannot get over it? Are you always in the past or in the future, thinking about what came and went or about something that hasn't happened yet? Have you over-identified with your glory days? Or are you feeling that you can't wait to get past this present life of yours so that at some moment in the future you can be (fill in the blank)? Are you spending your life right now on building a legacy, working hard to be remembered by unknown minds at some point in the future? Have you confused yourself with some moment that no longer is or isn't yet?

Are You Stuck in the Mirror of Language?

Are you feeling wounded by something somebody said to you or something you read about yourself? Are you calling yourself names, narrating your every misstep and/or triumph? Are you going to bat to protect your name? Are you caught up in some self-description, some "I am this" or "I am that" or "I am so-and-so" catchphrase? Are you wasting your life to be known as such-and-such word (for instance, "the first *this*" or "the first *that*")? Do you feel like you've gotten stuck on some word, like you choked on some realization that you are (fill in the blank)? In other words, have you confused yourself with a self-description?

Are You Stuck in the Inner Mirror (of Consciousness)?

Are you suffering from what you think about yourself? Do you have something in your mind about yourself that you can't seem to shrug off? Are you blaming yourself for thinking or feeling or imagining this or that? Are you incessantly looking for that one concrete, tangible, incontrovertible "thing" that you are? Are you caught up in chasing the lotus effect? Are you getting a bit perfectionistic about being informationally pure? Are you hung up on being 100 percent essence 100 percent of the time? Have you, in other words, confused yourself with some mind form, with something you thought, felt, sensed, imagined, perceived, and/or experienced?

five-step info/identity self-cleanse

Having triaged the mirror of identity you got trapped in, try the following five-step informational/identity self-cleanse.

1. Dis-identify from the information in question. Neti out the information that got under your skin. Browse through

the relevant neti-neti exercises in chapter 3. Choose the ones that seem most appropriate and do them.

2. Re-identify with your essential self. Engage in the am-ness meditation of your choice (see chapter 5) to complete the informational/identity self-cleanse.

3. Relax, to supplement the dis-identification/re-identification self-cleanse (see tips below).

4. Transcend the situation by forgiving the offender. This, however, is optional (see chapter 6).

5. Congratulate yourself on strengthening your lotus identity.

---

neti-doll ritual

Rituals help: they allow you to recruit the amazing effects of neural plasticity. Neuropsychologist Dr. Rick Hanson and neurologist Dr. Richard Mendius wrote: "Small positive actions…gradually build new neural pathways" (2009, 19). With this in mind, I'd like to offer you a lotus-effect-building self-detox ritual. I call it the *neti-doll ritual*. Recall my earlier reference to the Russian nesting dolls (*matryoshkas*) to make a key point that you are not a nothing. The neti-doll ritual that I propose is going to take the same idea in a slightly different direction. You'll see in a moment. But first, let's build a neti doll.

Purchase a cheap *matryoshka* set. Let's say it's a three-piece set: an outer doll, an inner doll, and the core doll. Paint all three dolls over (to cover up the designs) and label each doll as follows. On the outer doll, write: "I am not my circumstance, not my situations, not what I have, not what I earn, not what others think or feel about me, not my body, not my appearance, not my age, not my weight, not what I do, not my performance, not my behaviors." Label the inner doll: "I am not my mind, not my thoughts, not my feelings, not my sensations, not my self-concept, not my image of myself." And label the last, core doll: "My essence" (or "my spirit," "my soul," or "my consciousness"). Feel free to add adjectives: "my indescribable, indivisible essence."

Now that your neti doll is ready, here's the ritual itself. Let's say you experienced something that brought on an influx of information. This information challenges how you feel about yourself. You haven't been able to shrug off this impact, so here you are, with your neti doll. Follow this procedure:

1. **Retire:** Go to your room or some private space. Sit comfortably (in a half-lotus, if you're familiar with that posture), holding the neti doll in your hands (sitting in a chair would be fine as well).

2. **Locate:** Determine the level at which this information (within the neti doll) bothers you. For example, you might be ruminating about what so-and-so is thinking about you, so this would be located on the outer doll.

3. **Neti Out/Detox/Dis-identify:** Cleanse yourself of the impact the information is having on you. For example, if you've been ruminating about what so-and-so thinks about you, recognize that you are not the outer doll—you are not what others think. With this realization remove the outer doll and put it aside. While still holding the neti doll, take a few mindful breaths. Now, just as you are opening up the inner doll and putting that internal informational layer aside onto the floor, neti out (dis-identify with) whatever thoughts or feelings you have about the incident yourself.

4. **Re-identify:** So now you find yourself holding the solid, indivisible core doll. This is you. This is your cue to re-identify with your sense of am-ness. How? Just breathe for a while longer or use a favorite am-ness exercise from chapter 5. For example, plunge into the gap in between your thoughts or ask yourself: who am I? Repeat until you arrive at the sense of am-ness.

Tips: If you get a *matryoshka* set of four or more dolls, you can try to finish this neti doll meditation on a Sunyata-style note of emptiness. For instance, if you have a seven-piece *matryoshka*, you can paint over all the designs and label the layers as follows:

1. Not my circumstance

2. Not others' mind

3. Not what I have

4. Not my body

5. Not my mind

6. Not this, not that

End by putting the final (terminal, seventh) solid piece aside. As you dis-identify from each layer, including the one at which the information is eating at you, you eventually come to the last, "Not this, not that" doll. Except that this final neti doll isn't solid (remember that you've put the solid one aside). So, as you open this last neti doll, you end up with nothing, with a liberating informational void (or everything, depending on how you want to look at it). You're left with nothing that can be hurt or with all this reality to identify with—including the offending party. So, as you go through this process of removing the informational dirt and dis-identifying from various levels of identity, you eventually find yourself sitting with two half-pieces, a piece in each hand. If you'd like, you can inscribe the inside of one side of the final piece as "this" and the other as "that," to amplify the notion that you are neither this nor that.

Allow yourself to get creative. You can use different colors and shade from dark to light as you move inside the neti doll to communicate the idea of increasing clarity until you find yourself with the pristine transparence of what is as you open up the final "not this, not that" piece. Or, if you fancy the idea of having a solid, indivisible core at the end of this neti doll meditation, you can paint it as a lotus flower or a lotus seed. You can also stash fortune-cookie-style notes to yourself at each layer, with insights and quotations from previous meditations. Or you can just stash a couple of "notes to self" inside the last two-piece neti doll, using it as a kind of treasure trove. After all, remember that the self is a secret that cannot be told. Create whatever artistic happy ending to this information/identity detox that you like.

open-hands ritual

This is a simplified version of the neti-doll meditation, without any props except for a washable marker. With a washable marker write "not this" on the palm of one hand and "not that" on the palm of the other hand. Sit down with your hands facing upward but closed atop each knee. That's right: have your hands first *closed*. You'll see why in a second. Follow these steps:

1. While sitting with your hands turned up but closed atop each knee, bring up the informational predicament that you've gotten trapped in (think about what sullied your essential sense of self).

2. As you think about the information that has poisoned you, tightly clench both of your fists (remember to keep your hands facing upward). Allow the tension to build. Recall the situation vividly. Think hard about what happened and what it means to you about you. Get close to this informational dirt while clenching your fists at the same time.

3. When you're ready to let go of this tension, to free yourself from the hold that the information has on you, make a conscious choice to open your hands, one at a time, starting with the "not this" hand and following with the "not that" hand. As you open your hands, feel the tension drain and repeat to yourself: "Not this, not that."

4. Reinforce this release of toxic information with a few minutes of mindful breathing (or any other am-ness exercise of your choice) as you continue to sit with your hands open in acceptance of the reality of what is, just as it is.

5. When you're done, get up and mindfully wash your hands. Remember: not only are you not this or that, you're not even the "not this, not that" identity-detox mantra. Notice the water flow. Take a hint from it.

relaxation tip

A mental break isn't necessarily also a physical break. So, even if you have intellectually detoxed your identity from the given informational poison, your body might still be a phase behind. Consider one of the breath-focused exercises listed in chapters 5 or the relaxation exercise below.

wash it all away, one sip at a time

Drinking prompts us to become more mindful of our breathing. We reflexively slow down and time our sips so as not to choke. This preparation of the body for a drink becomes a kind of inadvertent relaxation of breath. It also helps that "parasympathetic fibers are spread throughout your lips; thus your lips stimulate PNS," the part of your nervous system that is responsible for relaxation (Hanson and Mendius 2009, 82).

Mindfully sip a glass of cold water. Feel the caressing, cleaning "hand" of the water as it strokes and soothes your throat. Imagine each sip purifying you. Notice this flow of water. Notice the flow of your mind. Find yourself on the bank of this river of experience. In between sips, ask yourself: who is this who is having this sip? Who is noticing these sensations, this informational flow, all this passing? Notice what remains after you ask. Welcome yourself back in all your pristine, unaffected perfection.

conclusion: give yourself permission to suffer

The mind is an information-processing system. As such, it is in the business of digestion, and, not unlike your stomach, sometimes it's irritated when things get too spicy. So, something happened, and now it's eating you as you are trying to digest it. The informational tug-of-war is on. No crisis here—it's the same old evolutionary game of the survival of the best-informed. Look: if you are alive and reading this, you've won this contest every time—you've eventually swallowed and processed every informational byte that reality served you.

Information processing, like food processing, is a metabolic process in the sense that it has its own pace and rate of digestion. Suffering is mulling over information, rumination. This kind of informational cud-chewing is a normal part of the digestive cycle. If you feel you have already masticated all the "musts" and "mustn'ts" out of this informational cud, then no need to chew on it again, just re-swallow it. Remember that in this war of digestion, your consciousness has found a way—each and every time—to stomach the information that it has been served. Remember that consciousness is self-cleaning. Find solace in the notion that there's never been a thought that has choked you to death.

As this river of consciousness runs its course, the ripple effects of the stone of judgment that disturbed the equanimity of your essence will soon smooth out and the silt of your resentment will eventually settle. All is fine as long as the river of your consciousness is flowing.

Here's a Russian information-processing digestion tip: "Morning is wiser than night" (*ootro vechera mudrenn'eye*). In other words, sleep on it. There's no shame in recruiting a bit of physiology to help your psychology along. It's the same process anyway! And remember to console yourself with the fact that whatever it is that you saw in the mirror of your consciousness, that too will pass. Take a tip from Bankei, a seventeenth-century Zen master: "The image doesn't stay in the mirror," particularly when you turn off the lights (Waddell 2000, 134). It's rare an informational cud survives until the next morning. In short, let go of this thought that you need to let go of this thought. Even the lotus closes for the night. Shed this desire to shed this suffering, and in so doing, watch the suffering slough off. Never mind the uninvited mind—it'll see itself out. See yourself in the morning just as you always are. And remember: the lotus of your consciousness is *self-cleaning*.

references

Austin, J. 1999. *Zen and the Brain: Toward an Understanding of Meditation and Consciousness.* Cambridge, MA: First MIT Press.

Barthlott, W., and C. Neinhuis. 1997. The purity of sacred lotus or escape from contamination in biological surfaces. *Planta* 202: 1–8.

Beckett, L. C. 1959. *Neti-Neti: Not This, Not That.* Bath, Somerset, UK: Pitman Press.

Bercholz, S., and S. C. Kohn. 1997. *An Introduction to the Buddha and His Teachings.* New York: Barnes & Noble Books.

Bertrand, J., R. Rappaport, and P. C. Sizonenko, eds. 1993. *Pediatric Endocrinology.* Baltimore: Williams & Wilkins.

Chopra, D. 2003. *The Spontaneous Fulfillment of All Desire: Harnessing the Infinite Power of Coincidence.* New York: Three Rivers Press.

Chalmers, D. 1995. Facing up to the problem of consciousness. *Journal of Consciousness Studies* 2(3):200–219.

Das, Surya. 2005. *Natural Radiance: Awakening to Your Great Perfection.* Boulder, CO: Sounds True, Inc.

de Bono, E. 1990. *Lateral Thinking: Creativity Step by Step.* New York: Harper & Row Publishers.

de Mello, A. 1984. *The Song of the Bird.* New York: Image Books.

de Nicolàs, A. 1976. *Meditations Through the Rg Veda: Four-Dimensional Man.* York Beach, ME: Nicolas-Hays.

Epstein, M. 1995. *Thoughts Without a Thinker: Psychotherapy from a Buddhist Perspective.* New York: MJF Books.

Fenner, P. 2002. *The Edge of Certainty: Dilemmas on the Buddhist Path.* York Beach, ME: Nicolas-Hays, Inc.

Fremantle, F. 2001. *Luminous Emptiness: Understanding the Tibetan Book of the Dead.* Boston: Shambhala.

Gyatso, Tenzin. 1988. *The Dalai Lama at Harvard.* J. Hopkins, trans, and ed. Ithaca, NY: Snow Lion Publications.

Halberstam, D. 1965. *The Making of a Quagmire: An Uncompromising Account of Our Precarious Commitment in South Vietnam.* New York: Random House.

Hanson, R., and R. Mendius. 2009. *Buddha's Brain: The Practical Neuroscience of Happiness, Love, and Wisdom.* Oakland, CA: New Harbinger Publications.

Harp, D. with N. Feldman. 1996. *The Three Minute Meditator.* New York: MJF Books.

Hopkins, J. 2006. Introduction to Mountain Doctrine: Tibet's Fundamental Treatise on Other-Emptiness and the Buddha Matrix, by Döl-bo-ba Shay-rap-gyel-tsen. J. Hopkins, trans. Ithaca, NY: Snow Lion Publications.

Hubben, W. 1997. *Dostoevsky, Kierkegaard, Nietzsche & Kafka.* New York: Touchstone.

Huxley, T. H. and W. J. Youmans. 1868. *The Elements of Physiology and Hygiene.* New York: Appleton & Co.

Johnson, W. 1982. *Riding the Ox Home: A History of Meditation from Shamanism to Science.* Boston: Beacon Press.

Jung, C. 1989. *Memories, Dreams, Reflections.* A. Jaffe, de. R. Winston and C. Winston, trans. New York: Vintage/Anchor Books.

Jung, C. 2009. *The Red Book.* S. Shamdasani, ed. S. Shamdasani, M. Kyburz, and J. Peck, trans. New York: W. W. Norton & Co.

Katz, J., ed. 2007. *One: Essential Writings on Nonduality.* Boulder, CO: Sentient Publications.

Keyes, K. Jr. 1975. *Handbook to Higher Consciousness.* 5th ed. Marina del Rey, CA: DeVorss & Company.

Kornfield, J. 2000. *After the Ecstasy, the Laundry.* New York: Bantam Books.

Krishnamurti, U. G. 2002a. *The Mystique of Enlightenment: The Radical Ideas of U. G. Krishnamurti*. R. Arms, ed. Boulder, CO: Sentient Publications.

———. 2002b. *Mind Is a Myth: Conversations with U. G. Krishnamurti*. T. Newland and S. P. Bansal, eds. New Delhi, India: Smriti Books.

Kundera, M. 1999. *The Unbearable Lightness of Being*. M. H. Heim, trans. New York: Harper Perennial.

Lee, I. 2005. *Human Technology: A Toolkit for Authentic Living*. Sedona, AZ: Healing Society.

Llinas, R. 2002. *I of the Vortex: From Neurons to Self*. Boston: The MIT Press.

Mantell, M. 1988. *Don't Sweat the Small Stuff: P.S. It's All Small Stuff*. Atascadero, CA: Impact Publishers.

National Geographic. 2009. *National Geographic: The Human Family Tree*. DVD. New York: National Geographic Studios.

Norbu, N. 1996. *Dzogchen: The Self-Perfected State*. A. Clemente, ed. Ithaca, NY: Snow Lion Publications.

Norbu, N. 2006. *Dzogchen Teachings*. J. Valby and A. Clemente, eds. Ithaca, NY: Snow Lion Publications.

Organ, T. W. 1970. *The Hindu Quest for the Perfection of Man*. Athens, OH: Ohio University Press.

Radhakrishnan, S., and C. A. Moore. 1957. *A Sourcebook in Indian Philosophy*. Princeton, NJ: Princeton University Press.

Ramanujan, A. K. 1973. *Speaking of Siva*. New York: Penguin Books.

Sach, J., and J. Faust. 2004. *The Everything Zen Book*. Avon, MA: Adams Media.

Schlitz, M., C. Vieten, and T. Amorok. 2007. *Living Deeply: The Art and Science of Transformation in Everyday Life*. Oakland, CA: New Harbinger Publications.

Shen-Miller, J., M. B. Mudgett, J. W. Schopf, S. Clarke, and R. Berger. 1995. Exceptional seed longevity and robust growth: Ancient Sacred Lotus from China. *American Journal of Botany* 82: 1367-80.

Shen-Miller, J., W. Schopf, G. Harbottle, R.j. Cao, S. Ouyang, K.-s. Zhou, J. R. Southon, and G.-h. Liu. 2002. Long-living lotus: Germination and soil [gamma]-irradiation of centuries-old fruits and cultivation, growth, and phenotypic abnormalities of offspring. *American Journal of Botany* 89:236-47.

Snelling, J. 1991. *The Buddhist Handbook: A Complete Guide to Buddhist Schools, Teaching, Practice, and History*. New York: Barnes & Noble.

Suzuki, Daisetz. 1953. Foreword to *Zen in the Art of Archery*, by Eugen Herrigel. New York: Pantheon Books.

Suzuki, D. T. 2006. *Zen Buddhism: Selected Writings of D. T. Suzuki*. New York: Doubleday.

Thich Nhat Hanh. 1999. *The Blooming of a Lotus: Guided Meditations for Achieving the Miracle of Mindfulness*. Boston: Beacon Press.

Thich Nhat Hanh. 2003. *Opening the Heart of the Cosmos: Insights on the Lotus Sutra*. Berkeley, CA: Parallax Press.

Time Magazine. 1951. Long-lived lotus. October 1.

Tzu, C. 2007. *Zhuangzi*. H. Hochsmann and Y. Guorong, trans. Longman Library of Primary Sources in Philosophy. D. Kolak, series ed. London: Pearson Publishing.

Tzu, C., H. Hochsmann, Y. Guorong, and D. Kolak. 2007. *Zhuangzi*. Longman Library of Primary Sources in Philosophy. London, UK: Pearson Publishing.

Vivekananda. 1993. *Living at the Source: Yoga Teachings of Vivekananda*. A. Myren and D. Madison, eds. Boston: Shambhala.

Waddell, N. 2000. *The Unborn: The Life and Teachings of Zen Master Bankei, 1622-1693*. New York: North Point Press.

Wilber, K. 1998. *The Essential Ken Wilber: An Introductory Reader*. Boston: Shambala.

Wittgenstein, L. 2007. *Tractatus Logico-Philosophicus*. C. K. Ogden, trans. New York: Cosimo Classics.

Yoon, C. K. 1996. Heat of lotus attracts insects and scientists. *New York Times*, October 1, C1.

Photo by John Colombo www.johncolombo.com

Pavel G. Somov, Ph.D., is a licensed psychologist in Pittsburgh, PA. He is author of *Eating the Moment* and *Present Perfect*.

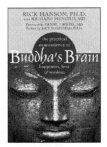